HOW SHALL THEY HEAR?

Missionary Messages by
Outstanding Christian Leaders

Compiled by

M. A. DARROCH, Th.D.

HOME DIRECTOR (from 1946 to 1958), SUDAN INTERIOR
MISSION

ZONDERVAN PUBLISHING HOUSE
GRAND RAPIDS, MICHIGAN

Printed in the United States of America

DEDICATION

This book is dedicated to the great host of missionaries laboring so faithfully in the "fields white unto harvest"—doing so much with so little. May God richly bless them and increase their numbers to the furtherance of the Gospel unto every tribe and creature.

I should also like to express my thanks to God and appreciation for a helpmeet in the work who has labored sacrificially hand in hand with me for more than a quarter of a century, with a burden to reach precious souls for Him.

How then shall they call on him in whom they have not believed? and how shall they believe in him of whom they have not heard? and how shall they hear without a preacher?

Romans 10:14

Believing that the most neglected preaching in the average pulpit is that of Missions, and with a view to increasing the interest in, and burden for, this vital ministry, we have felt led to gather these messages together in one volume and pray that it may be a contribution unto the furtherance of the Gospel in the regions beyond.

In proportion as a church, a pastor or a Christian layman is missionary-hearted, so God's hand of blessing will be upon that church, pastor or Christian layman. Why? Because Missions is God's revealed purpose for His own and those who will follow His program, as laid down in His word, can expect His blessing.

"Missionary-mindedness" is not sufficient. As many know about Christ but have never received Him as their own, so many Christians know about Missions but have never had the experience of a broken heart in behalf of the millions who have never heard the Gospel of our Lord Jesus Christ. It is with an earnest prayer that many may become *"missionary hearted"* through the reading of these messages that this book has been prepared. We need not only the *"mind of Christ"* but also the accompanying *heart compassion* of our blessed Lord, if the world is to be reached with His Gospel. "But when he saw the multitudes, he was moved with compassion on them, because they fainted, and were scattered abroad, as sheep having no shepherd. Then saith he unto his disciples, The harvest truly is plenteous, but the labourers are few. Pray ye therefore the Lord of the harvest that he will send forth labourers into his harvest" (Matt. 9:36-38).

The messages in this book are from the hearts of godly men whose ministries and lives have manifested a *missionary-heartedness*. They believe in Missions, they preach Missions, they participate, as well as lead, in a missionary program in their ministry for Him. We acknowledge with grateful appreciation the cooperation of these brethren and are thankful to God for them and for the work they are doing.

We believe that God is laying increasingly the burden of His heart upon some pastors. But one is heavy-hearted to realize how little real burden for missions is being preached from our pulpits today. It is a small percentage of the churches today that are carrying the tremendous load of foreign missions. Little wonder that Christianity seems to be losing ground daily in its race against increasing world population and the inroads of false religions. It is our earnest prayer that this book may be an instrument in God's hands of laying an increased burden upon the hearts of many, and that through it He may call (1) many young people to *GO* unto the regions beyond; (2) many of His servants to a faithful *preaching* of Missions and of leading in a missionary ministry; and (3) multitudes of Christians to *PRAY* and *GIVE* to fulfill His command to "Go into all the world" and to "preach the gospel to every creature."

"He which soweth sparingly shall reap also sparingly;

and he which soweth bountifully shall reap also bountifully."

Every creature could hear the Gospel in this generation, if every Christian were faithful in his responsibility.

"He is not willing that any should perish" — Are we, His representatives, His ambassadors in this heathen world, willing? Am I? Are you?

We count it a great privilege and honor to be in this manner a co-worker with the great host of faithful missionaries of the Cross. If we can but help to sharpen another's weapons for the fight, or carry a cup of cold water to those who are bearing the burden and heat of the day, we will rejoice and do rejoice.

M. A. DARROCH

CONTENTS

I

THE CRISIS IN CHRISTIAN MISSIONS
HAROLD OCKENGA

. . . All power is given unto me in heaven and in earth. Go ye therefore, and teach all nations, baptizing them in the name of the Father, and of the Son, and of the Holy Ghost: Teaching them to observe all things whatsoever I have commanded you: and, lo, I am with you alway, even unto the end of the world (Matthew 28:18).

In 1933 I was touring eastern Europe preaching the gospel along the Russian border (by means of interpreters my messages were translated into Yiddish, Russian and Polish). In Stolin our meetings were scheduled for a theater. Placards had been placed throughout the town and when the evening came we made our way across the cobblestone street toward a theater. We were surrounded by the members of the little local church and by a large assembly of uncouth and dirty people also going to the theater. Arriving, we found both the inside and outside of the theater packed. So much so, that the people could no longer sit in the seats and had to stand crushed close to one another by the impact of their fellows. The platform itself was occupied by the church. The people in the pews were atheists, unbelievers, Jews, members of the Greek Orthodox Church, members of the Roman Catholic Church, and others. Following my sermon there was a great disturbance which we feared might turn into a riot.

HAROLD J. OCKENGA is pastor of the Park Street Church of Boston, Massachusetts. During his ministry here the church has become one of the outstanding missionary churches in the country. Their missionary giving has reached over $200,000 each year and their annual missionary conference is known throughout the land.

9

The priests were attempting to prohibit any demonstrations on the part of those who were convinced by the sermon. Finally, surrounded by the native Christians, we left the theater and went to the little one-story hotel.

As we were about to enter the building two soldiers stepped up to us and asked for a word. They were soldiers of the Polish Army. We entered the hotel, turned to the reception room, the darkness of which was lighted by one lamp hanging from the ceiling and the bareness of which was broken by a table and four chairs. I motioned to the spokesman for the soldiers to be seated across from me at the table. His friend was seated at my left. My interpreter was on the right and a Russian pastor stood in the shadows.

The officer began: "I heard you in the theater tonight and have come to speak to you. I have found that every man has some baggage which he carries with him and which he may give to another. I have come to see what baggage you have for us. I was brought up in the Greek Orthodox church, but now have no religion at all. I have watched the rise of Communism in Russia and fear it here in Poland. It is a powerful movement, a religion which makes demands upon the individual but which offers him much."

While the officer was speaking, I was studying him. He had a high forehead, a finely chiseled face, long, aristocratic fingers, an immaculate uniform, a physically strong body, and unusually clear eyes. I realized that I was listening to an intelligent man and I coveted him for Christ.

He went on: "You told us of Christianity, of redemption, of a new life for individuals and for society and I believe you have something to say to us. I am ready to listen."

Then I began and through the interpreter preached Christ to him — from the great doctrines of revelation through the redemption of Calvary and on into the Christian church and society. I concluded with a personal testimony of what Jesus Christ had done for me in saving me from my sins and assuring me of salvation and in giving me eternal life. Then I challenged him to accept Christ.

Without a single word he stood erect, pushing his chair backward, and thrust his hand out across the table. I also stood and took that hand in a firm grasp realizing that he had made his decision. Then I turned and took his companion by the hand and asked the interpreter to request them to kneel in prayer, which we did. After our period of prayer, we arose from our knees, expressed our gratitude to God for the decision of these officers and watched the Russian pastor give literature to them. After a few final words, when they were about to depart, the first officer turned to me and said, "Communism is making its claim upon Poland. Christianity is also challenging Poland. Whichever one makes its message a flame of fire will win Poland." And with that he went out.

Many times those words have echoed in my mind and heart. Where is Poland today — in which orbit of the world? Where is China? Will Germany, France, Spain, Italy and Africa be in that orbit tomorrow? Only one obstacle stands in the way of their likewise coming under the control of materialistic Communism. That obstacle is not capitalism, for even capitalistic America may be subject to a complete revolution overnight.

There are two schools of thought concerning the Communist revolution. One is the Bolshevik school under the leadership of Lenin which believed in violence as a means of the revolution of the proletariat to establish its dictatorship. This occurred in Russia. But the Karl Kautsky school of Germany believed in establishing the revolution by legislation. Once the Communist Party should win the power by the franchise it then would end all democratic procedure and establish a dictatorship with a firm hand. That possibility could be fulfilled in America. Then there will be no passports, no freedom of speech, no freedom of worship, no freedom of propagandizing and then the era of missions will be over.

Today, however, the door is still open and no man can shut it until God wills that it be shut. Is the Gospel in your heart a living flame of fire? What part will you play in the great decision of this critical age to keep the rest of the world from becoming like Poland? The only answer to that question rests in the missionary enterprise as represented by the Great Commission given by the Lord Jesus Christ.

I. The Greatest Possible Authority for Missions

After His resurrection and probably at that first missionary conference meeting on a mountain in Galilee and attended by five hundred disciples, the Lord Jesus said, "All authority is given unto me in heaven and in earth." Whatever is to be done in evangelizing the world must be done under the sovereignty of Christ. To this St. Paul called attention in his missionary speech at Athens when he declared that God had commanded all men to repent because "He hath appointed a day, in which he will judge the world in righteousness by that man whom he hath ordained; whereof he hath given assurance unto all men, in that he hath raised him from the dead." All the missionary texts of the New Testament are centered in Christ. It is declared, "It behooved Christ to suffer, and to rise from the dead the third day: that repentance and remission of sins should be preached in his name among all nations" and "Ye shall be witnesses unto me both in Jerusalem, and in all Judaea, and in Samaria, and unto the uttermost part of the earth."

Missions, therefore, are grounded in the person of Christ. We must have a Christology that includes His eternal and pre-existent person, His incarnation as second person of the Trinity in human flesh, His supernatural power to do miracles while on earth, His authoritative teaching, His atoning death, His bodily resurrection, His present authority in the kingdom and His future position as judge. Only a Christology grounded in God the Son is sufficient to authorize the missionary enterprise. Therefore, the examples of missionary preaching given in the book of Acts all possess this high Christology.

The sovereignty of Christ as judge of the world was granted as a result of His work. Since He died for the redemption of the world, He reasonably ought to determine the destiny of the world. During His earthly sojourn He was tempted in all points like as we are, apart from sin, and He carried His identification with us to the tasting of death for every man. For this reason He is given sovereignty. Paul declares that the same Christ who had emptied Himself and was obedient unto death has been highly exalted and given a name which is above every name: that at the name of Jesus every knee should bow. Christ's own testimony connects His suffering with His glory in the post-resurrection appearances and is drawn from Moses and the prophets. An example of this is found in Psalm 22, which is a prophecy of the suffering Messiah and about whom it is said, "For the kingdom is the Lord's: and he is the governor among the nations."

That sovereignty is exercised by Christ now as governor of the nations, as defending His church, as He simultaneously reveals, redeems and rules as Prophet, Priest and King. Therefore, all authority belongs unto Him. This authority initiates the missionary enterprise.

The sphere of Christ's activity needs to be emphasized today, in the light of the teaching which confines His ministry to intercession during the present age. The book of Revelation was written to give comfort to God's people in an age of persecution and suffering from the world and to continue to give that comfort during the entire age until Jesus Christ comes again.

An analysis of the book of Revelation reveals seven visions of Jesus Christ. We are convinced that these seven visions of Christ portray His present activities, each of which will have a culminating effect eschatologically. First, Christ is seen in the midst of the seven candlesticks, judging His church. That position He exercises through the entire age. The angels of the churches are within His hands and His authority is exercised over those churches both by way of comfort, admonition and judgment.

Next, Christ is seen seated in heaven as the Lion of the Tribe of Judah and as a Lamb slain, worthy to open the seven seals. There we see Him as the Lord of Providence determining the events of history which involve His church. Third, we see Him as Priest at the golden altar interceding for His people and offering up the prayers of His people. Fourth, we see Him as the Prophet holding the little book in His hand and revealing the future. Fifth, He is seen as the Deliverer of Zion, eternally securing the salvation of His people. Sixth, He is manifested as the coming King who will judge the nations. Finally, we see Him as the Judge on the Great White Throne exercising judgment over the quick and the dead. Here is a picture of the activity and sovereignty of Christ, some of which is being exercised today and some of which will only be fully exercised in the consummation. All that we are is in His hands. He is the defender and vindicator of His church.

Submission to Christ, therefore, is the beginning of missions. Unless we recognize that through Christ and Him only we are saved, we may have no part in the missionary enterprise. Through Christ and Christ alone comes forgiveness of sin, righteousness with God and possession of eternal life. Through Christ alone we can know the plan of God for our life. He declared, "If any man will do his will, he shall know of the doctrine." Christ is the touchstone of our knowledge of God's will or plan and it is necessary for us to know and to prove what is the good, acceptable and perfect will or plan of God for our own lives. This means a total surrender to Christ. Through Christ alone we may consider the missionary cause.

A surrender to Christ will involve obedience. Many duties are declared in the Scripture to obligate the Christian when he accepts Christ as Saviour and Lord. One of these is, "Go." It is absolutely essential that we should know why we ought not to go if we are not to obey that command. Unless God has a particular place for us in the division of labors within the body of Christ which excludes our going, we ought to consider the obligation resting upon us.

II. THE GREATEST POSSIBLE FIELD OF ENDEAVOR

The Lord Jesus said, "Go ye therefore, and teach all nations." The field of endeavor is the world and the need of the nations of the world is appalling.

Let us pause to consider the need in America and to recognize it. America is aggressively rejecting God. It may be startling for you to know that the United Nations organization lists its members according to religion and the United States is listed officially as pagan. It would be easy for us to prove that point from the immorality, juvenile delinquency, drunkenness, graft, dishonesty and break-up of the family, which has now reached thirty-three per cent of the marriages, if we so desired. But it is not our purpose to indict America. America has had its light. America can know the will of God if it will know it. Enough evangelical radio broadcasts are carried on in America every week for every man, woman and child to hear the Gospel. Moreover, American cities and towns have had the Gospel for decades, even if they are at present turning from it. America's judgment will be worse than the judgment of the heathen world. It is a principle of divine judgment that nations shall be judged according to relative enlightenment. Jesus said, ". . . that servant, which knew his Lord's will, and prepared not himself, neither did according to his will, shall be beaten with many stripes. But he that knew not, and did commit things worthy of stripes, shall be beaten with few stripes. For unto whomsoever much is given, of him shall much be required . . ." (Luke 12:47,48).

I would rather have lived and died in heathen darkness and to stand before the judgment of God than I would to live and die in America rejecting the light which we have. The heathen will fare far better. The question before us is not the need of America but the question of where God wants me to be. Does He want my testimony in America or does He want it on the foreign field? Personally, I once was a member of the Student Volunteers, but I find myself as minister of Park Street Church because that is the missionary field in which God wants me to labor, for from there He is sending out His missionaries (numbering 131 on the present roster), for there He is holding a testimony in the midst of an area under the influence of all kinds of non-evangelical religions.

Pause, therefore, to consider the foreign field, beginning at Europe. On a recent visit to England I received an impression of the vast need of that nation. Only ten per cent of the entire population belongs to the church and less than five per cent attends church. According to travelers in France the situation is far worse. Visitors from the British Isles tell us that in some cities of a hundred thousand, not a hundred young people will be found in church on a given Sunday. Nevertheless, those same cities are feeling the impact of the tremendous revival in London of 1954. In the whole European field, no doubt the neediest country is Germany. The ideology of Nazism is largely gone. The strength of Protestantism is broken. Into the vacuum are rushing ideas from Communistic Russia and from Catholic Italy, while evangelical Christendom stands idly by and ignorant of the fact that the future of Europe is now being decided in that nation. Europe is one vast mission field calling for the keenest brains of American youth.

Japan is wide open. Bernard Iddings Bell declared at the explosion of the atomic bomb, that missions were done for a century in the Orient, but Japan has disproved that statement and has been ready to receive the Gospel from the victor whose material might and efficiency she admires. Shintoism is broken. Buddhism is helpless. And the Japanese are floundering without any true religion. There, mission work of all kinds prospered under G.I. leadership until mission boards caught the vision of the great opportunity in Japan.

India is passing through its transition toward autonomy. The general population is awakening. Revolution has recently occurred and readjustment is necessary. In all this the Christian message will have a tremendous importance. In the Orient, the hour of Christian missions has struck. The door is open.

Africa presents a new challenge, for never were facilities available for reaching those continents as they are available by roads, air travel and radio, today. Great is the debt which the whites owe Africa. Through the slavery of the long past centuries the black man has been exploited to satisfy the white man's greed and lust. No section of the world has been outraged by the white man such as Africa, and yet there are also sections of Africa which the white man has not reached, namely, the primitive, infected, cowering Africa of the native where disease, starvation, ignorance and fear stalk down its long grass trails from village to village. Day and night the natives are preyed upon with nothing to remove their curse. Northern Africa was once under the control of Christian thought. Where once the songs and hymns of the church and the messages of the fathers were heard, Mohammedanism has moved in and now a large section of Africa is Moslem. Along with Mohammedanism comes a resurgent and aggressive Catholicism making its claims through those areas under the leadership of Catholic nations. Thus Christian America is faced with the challenge of pouring in missionaries where the testimony may still be heard.

Never will I forget the recent visit of Louis Browne to my office where after we exchanged certain personal reminiscences, he suddenly burst into a flood of tears over the indifference of America to the Gospel and over the receptivity of the people of the Congo to Christ. Mr. Browne wept tears of longing to return to his people in Africa.

What shall I say of South America and Latin America in which secularism is rampant, where Roman Catholicism is rising in persecution and yet in which Protestantism is having tremendous successes? I use in illustration only the West Indies Mission which in twenty short years has had nearly one hundred thousand converts and established over a hundred churches manned by native pastors and Christians. Wherever you look in the world you will see mankind sick, rotting, rancorous and bitter, affecting every other part of mankind. Does the picture not stir your heart?

In the face of this Commission to the nations, consider what has been done in this relatively important work. Statistics tell us that there are no more than thirty-five thousand missionaries engaged in the wonderful work of winning souls, of testifying to the millions, of witnessing to Christ in the world. That means in the non-Christian populations of the world there is not a missionary to each hundred thousand people, whereas in America we have a minister for every five hundred people, at least.

I would hesitate to compare the amount of money spent for missions with the amount spent on liquor, cosmetics, cigarettes and other unnecessary things. Without the primary motive of saving perishing men, for eternity, young people will never face this tremendous challenge. The secondary motives of medicine, sanitation, education, economics, farming, abundant living are insufficient to drive men out from their home country, their friends, their families and their opportunities, to go into the mission fields. Only the necessity of preaching the Gospel will ever compel us to go. For this reason, the vitiating theology of liberalism has cut the nerve of missions. Let your sense of balance, of fairness, of responsibility, as a Christian govern your thinking even if the Great Commission does not.

Every Christian has a responsibility to these hundreds of millions who never hear about Christ. If these people are lost, because they have not heard the Gospel, and if we have the Gospel, and do not take it to them, then most certainly we, too, will be lost because we did not believe in Christ and accept Christ's authority. We are not lost because of what we have done or what we have not done, but our failure to go will reveal that we did not believe Jesus Christ nor accept His authority in our lives. Christ Himself said, "Many will say to me in that day, Lord, Lord, have we not prophesied in thy name? and in thy name have cast out devils? and in thy name have done many wonderful works? And then will I profess unto them, I never knew you: depart from me, ye that work iniquity" (Matthew 7:22,23).

Remember that God is just and in the light of such justice how could you stand at Christ's judgment seat and be justified with millions in hell because you did not carry the message to them? This is the motive which gave the great impetus to foreign missions in the past. When men get this vision of the judgment to come, and of responsibility, they go. That is why Paul went ever on and on and on. That is why he would not build upon another man's foundation. That is why William Carey worked at his cobbler's bench with the tears running down his face and with prayers in his heart for the heathen until he could start the modern missionary enterprise. That is why Hudson Taylor with indefatigable zeal went throughout China. That is why David Brainerd prayed and labored himself to an early grave that he might bring the Gospel to the heathen Indians. That is why Adoniram Judson refused the post as pastor of Park Street Church in order that he might minister to the Karens in Burma. If men are lost, then we must *go* until the last one has heard the Gospel.

III. THE GREATEST POSSIBLE TASK IN THE WORLD

Christ commissioned us to "teach all nations, baptizing them in the name of the Father, and of the Son, and of the Holy Ghost, teaching them to observe all things whatsoever I have commanded you."

I received a letter from a professor of one of America's greatest educational institutions (he has a daughter on the mission field), saying, "If the heathen are to be judged in the full light of God's justice and mercy, the question often arises 'Why try to convert them, why not leave them alone? — they are well enough off for time and eternity.' Many of those who are unsympathetic with the missionary motive stand behind this question and assertion. Sometime I wish you would preach a sermon on the general subject, 'Why Missions?'" Why indeed? Why should we as a church spend $215,000.00 this year in supporting 131 missionaries when we could use it in so many other things at home? Why should some of my people give as high as 25% or 35% of their income to missions and go without summer homes and automobiles? Why should one of the young men in our congregation give so largely to missions that he had to sell his automobile? Why should we expose our children to the missionary cause? Why indeed if they are well enough off alone?

The Bible answers that question for us by telling us that we must make disciples of all nations because all men are lost. John tells us in speaking of Christ, "That was the true light, which lighteth every man that cometh into the world." Paul declared, ". . . the invisible things of him from the creation of the world are clearly seen, being understood by the things that are made, even His eternal power and Godhead; so that they are without excuse" (Romans 1:20) and ". . . when the Gentiles, which have not the law, do by nature the things contained in the law, these, having not the law, are a law unto themselves: Which shew the work of the law written in their hearts, their conscience also bearing witness and their thoughts the meanwhile excusing or else accusing one another" (Romans 2:14,15). From this it is evident that the heathen possess a law of God and a knowledge of that law. This also is declared in Romans 5:12 when Paul expounds the power of death over men because all have sinned, even though sin is not imputed where there is no law. Obviously the moral law of God was not revealed in the Ten Commandments until Mount Sinai, but men possessed knowledge of the law of God from general revelation before that time which accounts for the similar codes held by Hammurabi and the Babylonians.

Every man has that light or knowledge and every man has rejected that light and broken that law and confirmed his inner depravity and sinfulness. Therefore, "Death passed upon all men, for all have sinned." This is declared by Isaiah: "All we like sheep have gone astray. We have turned every one to his own way," and by the Psalmist, "There is none righteous, no not one. There is none that seeketh God. There is none that doeth good," and by Paul in the first three chapters of Romans.

Therefore every man is under the wrath and condemnation of God. He is treasuring up for himself indignation against the day of wrath and is described as perishing whether with a knowledge of the Mosaic law or without that knowledge. "If our gospel be hid, it is hid to them that are lost."

We are to make disciples of all nations because God hath set a day to judge the world in righteousness. Consider what that judgment means from the Biblical description of hell and death and of the lake of fire and brimstone. When a righteous God makes inquisition for sin, men are found sinners and condemned to eternal torment because they have not repented and believed on Christ, will your hands be clean? Will you have obeyed Christ and carried the Gospel to as many as you could or will you, too, be responsible? Paul speaks of this day when God shall judge the secrets of men by Jesus Christ "according to my gospel."

We are to make disciples of all nations because Christ is set to be the judge. We have already referred to this earlier in treating of His sovereignty. Now we must realize that men will be judged according to their attitude toward Christ, toward "that man." Hence, they must know about Him as Saviour or must meet Him as Judge. The Scripture unequivocally declares that "Neither is there salvation in any other: for there is none other name under heaven given among men, whereby we must be saved." If any man is saved, it will not be because of his works but because of Jesus Christ who is the revealer of our hearts.

How shall we make disciples? By preaching. Thus the importance of publishing the glad tidings of good things. Paul says, "Whosoever shall call upon the name of the Lord shall be saved." "How then shall they call upon him in whom they have not believed? And how shall they believe in him of whom they have not heard? And how shall they hear without a preacher? And how shall they preach, except they be sent? As it is written, How beautiful are the feet of them that preach the gospel of peace, and bring glad tidings of good things" (Romans 10:14,15). This is the divine order, calling, believing, hearing, preaching, being sent. Thus we must begin with sending and preaching and expect the conversion of men. The reason is this, that the Gospel, the message of Calvary and the work of the Holy Spirit, persuades the will of man and enables him to believe. A man who comes into this world with a corrupt nature and a depraved will may be turned by the Gospel to repent, confess and believe. Thus we are not only to preach but baptize, to bring men to a committal of faith and a public profession of faith in the triune God. A clean breach method is the Biblical method of evangelism. We have no hope of converting the world, but we have a great hope of witnessing to the nations and calling out a people for His name.

Therefore we do go to make disciples and to teach them to observe all things whatsoever Christ commandeth. This is a tremendous program involving the doctrines of Christianity, the ethics of Christian living, and the understanding of the truth of the remnant. The question always arises as to whether missions should be extensive or intensive. Should we go to the last tribe, nation and people before we attempt to teach? Now Christ obviously placed these two objectives in correlation. We are not to think for a moment that going from people to people as Francis Xavier did, teaching them the Lord's Prayer, the Ten Commandments and a few other things, will convert them. We are both to make disciples and to teach.

IV. The Greatest Possible Assurance of Success

To this commission Christ added the words, "And lo I am with you alway." Frankly, that is supernaturalism and it is against the supernatural that the modern age rebels. We are witnessing the attack of naturalism to this missionary program which attack is based upon a theology of naturalism. Evolutionary naturalism has captured one field after another until it has entered the realm of theology and there it claims that given certain circumstances, man will naturally develop a religion which is thus a deterministic phenomenon called by different names at different places. Religion has nothing supernatural about it at all. God is the social process and man is the chief end of the process; ethical monotheism and social righteousness represent the development of the religious consciousness of a people, and the state of the various religions merely represents various people's response to different stimuli.

From this comes a relativism affecting history, conscience and truth, until morals, religion, philosophy and politics are reduced to temporary manifestations in certain sets of circumstances. Humanism thus has no final message of truth or salvation or God or self or sin or righteousness to give to the world except the dogmas of the inherent goodness of man and inevitable progress, both now debunked by two World Wars.

Naturalism interprets Missions in an entirely different way than does supernaturalism. Missions does not consist of going to preach to the lost, to declare the Gospel to perishing men, but to share something which we possess. The new attitude is to exchange on an equal level the good in all religions. Just as foreign nations receive missionaries, so we are to receive missionaries here and to be tolerant of all teachings accepting what is good in them all. We are never to talk about salvation of a soul, but about social betterment, literacy, good government and other humanistic improvements.

The influence of humanism on Missions has been great. It has cut the nerve of the missionary enterprise due to the loss of faith in the essential truth of Christianity. In the very proportion that liberal Christianity has gained dominion in the church the missionary work has declined and the missionary emphasis has been removed. This was proved by the teaching and facts included in the work "Rethinking Missions."

The antidote to such an attack is faith in the supernaturalism of Jesus. This is established in the resurrection. It is the resurrection which was the polemic of the missionary preaching of the book of Acts. It was to the resurrection that Paul referred when he advised Timothy to stir up the gift of God that was within him. In the midst of the skepticism of the university centers of his day, where Timothy's flaming heart might grow cold, Paul reminded him, among other things, to "remember that Jesus Christ of the seed of David was raised from the dead according to our gospel." When a man stands face to face with that resurrection, he has an intellectual proof of the supernatural. This may be experienced in the present gift of the Holy Spirit. The resurrected, glorified, living Christ shed His Spirit abroad on the Day of Pentecost and that Spirit may be received by the individual today. Through Him, he shares the presence of Christ. Thus the missionary is never alone in his suffering, his burdens, his obstacles and all that he must face. The Holy Spirit is God in us as Christ was Immanuel or God with us when He was here upon earth. Such a truth and experience brings a satisfaction anywhere

Such supernaturalism is exhibited in the power of the Holy Ghost whom Jesus promised to His disciples. That power is to live, to preach, and to die. Under His anointing, His equiping, His blessing we may do that which God wills that we shall do. And hereby men shall come to know our Christ.

Beware, then, of the anomaly of going without Christ. Christ is with us when we are in Christ or born again by His Spirit, when we receive the forgiveness of sins, righteous standing before God, and life by His Spirit. This new life of victory, power and blessing is ours in the proportion that we are filled with the Holy Spirit. The new vision of the world is given with the throne view of Christ — and that is the missionary view.

This the Lord tells us is the program till the end of the age. It is His program. If we want blessing, we must be engaged in His program. The age may be short and while it continues atheistic naturalism seems to be gaining ground. We have no hope for the conversion of the world as held by men such as Charles G. Finney and Charles Hodge. The Bible gives no evidence of that. We stand today in an atomic age which holds an impending sword of Damocles over our heads and in which the threat of Revelation 6 to 16 may be fulfilled at any time. This is the acceptable time of the age of grace and it may end at any moment. This is the hour of respite when a chance is given to the church to evangelize the world and to carry the Gospel to the nations. What is to be done must be done now.

Is Christianity in your heart a flame of fire that will conquer the nations? If not, God has no other plan. "Who knoweth whether thou art come to the kingdom for such a time as this?"

II

THE SCORN OF JOB
William Culbertson

It is on my heart to share with you some missionary thoughts based upon a portion of the Word of God which at first blush may seem rather strange indeed, for the text will be found in the book of Job.

You may recall that the larger part of the book of Job is devoted to a setting forth of the discourses of Job's friends and Job's replies to them. The portion at which we shall look today is taken from the final reply of Job. It is a tremendous avowal of innocency, in which Job turns aside the thrust of his friend that he must have committed some heinous sin, to suffer the way he was suffering. In Chapters 29 through 31 of the book of Job, that final reply of Job is recorded for us. Before the book is concluded, he will speak again; but that will be after God has revealed Himself and Job comes in contrition and repentance to his God.

I should like to quote a paragraph from Chapter 31 of the book of Job, beginning at the sixteenth verse. Job is speaking. He is speaking to Eliphaz, Bildad and Zophar, his friends.

> If I have withheld the poor from their desire,
> Or have caused the eyes of the widow to fail,
> Or have eaten my morsel myself alone,
> And the fatherless hath not eaten thereof;

William Culbertson is the well-known and beloved President of Moody Bible Institute and has traveled extensively himself through mission fields. Moody Bible Institute has trained and sent forth more young people to the mission fields of the world than any other school and continues to do so each year. Much emphasis is placed upon foreign and home missions in all of its training program.

(For from my youth he was brought up with me,
  as with a father,
And I have guided her from my mother's womb;)
If I have seen any perish for want of clothing,
Or any poor without covering;
If his loins have not blessed me,
And if he were not warmed with the fleece of
  my sheep;
If I have lifted up my hand against the fatherless,
When I saw my help in the gate:
Then let mine arm fall from my shoulder blade,
And mine arm be broken from the bone.
For destruction from God was a terror to me,
And by reason of his highness I could not endure.

Thus does Job avow that in his heart was no uncharitableness, but rather the warmness of his soul showed in the beneficence of his hand.

Now in this word of protestation, Job uses an expression which tremendously intrigues me. In verse 17 he speaks this way: "If I have eaten my morsel alone" — if, out of that which God has granted me, I have given nothing to others who, in desperate need, are all about me — "Then, let mine arm fall from my shoulder-blade, and mine arm be broken from the bone; for destruction from God was a terror to me. . ."

"If I have eaten my morsel alone. . ." You and I live in a land of plenty; and it is a land of plenty, not only in physical and material blessings, but also in spiritual privilege. You and I have the Book of God; we enjoy the Church of God. The blessings of God to us are manifold. The Word of God itself sets forth figuratively its ministry to us as bread for our need, as the satisfying portion of our spirits. May I ask, are we eating our morsel alone?

I recognize the impropriety of the word "morsel," for a banqueting table, lavishly spread, has been put before us, and thereof we eat and eat plenteously. But I wonder if we eat alone; whether our minds and hearts have ever reached beyond the things of time and sense, beyond our own personal limited environment; whether something of God's great desire for perishing multitudes all over the world who stand in need of the bread of God — I say, I wonder whether that thought has ever reached into our hearts and become a motivating part in our lives.

A bishop of the Irish Church some years ago took hold of this little word from Job, and wrote a poem. It reads like this:

"If I have eaten my morsel alone!"
    The Patriarch spoke in scorn;
What would he think of the Church were he shown
    Heathendom, huge, forlorn,
Godless, Christless, with soul unfed,
    While the Church's ailment is fullness of bread,
Eating her morsel alone?

"I am debtor alike to the Jew and the Greek,"
    The Mighty Apostle cried;
Traversing continents, souls to seek,
    For the love of the Crucified,
Centuries, centuries since have sped;
    Millions are famishing; we have bread,
But we eat our morsel alone.

"Even of those who have largest dower
    Shall heaven require the more."
Ours is affluence, knowledge, power,
    Ocean from shore to shore;
And East and West in our ears have said,
    "Give us, give us your Living Bread,"
Yet we eat our morsel alone.

"Freely, as ye have received, so give,"
    He bade, who has given us all.
How shall the soul in us longer live,
    Deaf to their starving call,
For whom the blood of the Lord was shed
    And His body broken to give them bread,
If we eat our morsel alone?

Would you think with me of three things? Would you face the famishing world? Would you think of our failure? And would you consider finally, what we can do about it?

I. The Famishing World

First of all, the famishing world. Some of us know personally that great, stalwart saint of God, missionary statesman, Dr. Charles E. Scott, Presbyterian minister and missionary in the land of China years ago. It was Dr. Scott who emphasized and underlined for us that six-sevenths of the world is without Christ. It is hard for us who live in a so-called Christian land to understand what that means. We have our church, we have our Bible, we have our family. We may be tempted to think that all the world is like our world. But it isn't.

Men are without Christ. Now let us not argue that men without Christ are lost. Let us not debate philosophical questions. The Word of God is crystal clear; and we are Christians, we believe the Word of God. The Lord Jesus Christ is our Saviour and our Lord; and that blessed Book of God which gives us the revelation of the Christian message is the same Book of God which affirms, "Neither is there salvation in any other; for there is none other name under heaven given among men, whereby we must be saved" (Acts 4:12).

It is this same Book which makes clear, "He that hath the Son hath life; and he that hath not the Son, hath not life" (I John 5:12). It was our blessed Saviour Himself who said, "I am the way . . . . . no man cometh unto the Father, but by me" (John 14:6).

Multitudes do not have that message, and therefore do not know that Saviour. A friend of mine, the head of a missionary society, gave a table of statistics concerning the incompleted missionary task. After a good deal of careful research, he came up with this answer: that in seven large areas, there are at least 1,000 tribes without the Gospel: 350 of them in Africa, 300 of them in South America, 100 of them in India, 70 in Siberia, and 60 each in China, the Philippines and Indo-China. Men without Christ!

Some of you may know the work of the Wycliffe Translators, a notable work indeed, with the purpose that people should have the Word of God in their own language — which means the reducing to writing of a language in many instances, and then the translation of the Book of God into that particular tongue. Mr. Cameron Townsend, the head of that work, affirmed at the beginning of last year that, according to their statistics as they have been able to make surveys, there are over 2,000 tribes that have nothing of the Word of God in their own language.

It may interest you to know that great strides have been taken; and perhaps you are acquainted with the fact that the Bible, in whole or in part, is printed in over 1,000 different languages and tongues. Of that number, only 200 have the whole Bible; you and I take the whole Bible for granted. Only 200 have the whole Bible! 200 more have the whole New Testament. 500 have less than the New Testament. 100 have less than one book.

How shall they hear without a preacher? How shall they preach unless they are sent? How shall these people know unless they have the Word of God given to them? There is a world without the Saviour, with little or no opportunity to come to Him. Over a billion souls without the Lord, many without even a word concerning the Lord. How can we sit back? How can we remain complacent? How can we be at ease in Zion, when the final word of our Lord ere He departed from His Church was, "Go ye into all the world and preach the gospel"?

Please do not misunderstand me. I am not a pessimist. I am not coming to you in any morbid spirit at all. Thank God, there is the spirit of advance in the atmosphere. But we must bend our efforts the more; we must know what it means to live as disciples more than we ever have. For under the blessing of God, this situation in which there is a world without the living bread can be turned into a world having the living bread, if you and I as Christians mean business with the Lord. These souls are going out into eternity. One every second, we are told, leaves this world in death and many of them never having heard of the Saviour.

Have you ever attended a funeral where there has been hopelessness, darkness? Oh, my friend, consider the world — that heathen world, which in population is increasing in number, both in an absolute and a relative sense. We dare not wait until tomorrow.

II. Our Failure

The famishing world! Think for a moment, if you will, of our failure. We are told that in the United States of America there is at least one minister for every 1100 people, probably less than 1100. Now granted that is a large parish; but it is nothing compared to the great parishes that our missionaries have to face. Those of us who have had the privilege of visiting with them, of being with them on their stations, of sharing with them something of their heart-burden; we know that it is the rule that the missionary will say, "Oh, that there were many more, for I cannot reach the multiplied thousands for which I am responsible." And some of them go on an itinerant ministry, and stay a few days and press on. There is no one to care for the converts and lead them on. And others centralize their work in a place, and try to reach out from that center, but it is all so hopeless unless our forces are made larger.

III. What We Can Do About It

Our failure! Is God saying anything to you about that? You say, "Well, they are not immediately in my presence. I can forget them." Ah, that is the tragedy! That is the thing that breaks the heart of the foreign missionary and of the Christian minister at home, the worker who senses something of the desperate need of the world. We are satisfied, sufficient. Well cared for are we. Would you let that word of Job penetrate into your innermost soul? — "If I have eaten my morsel alone." It was unthinkable so far as Job was concerned. God grant it should be equally unthinkable for you!

Finally, what are we to do about it? The answer I would give is simplicity itself — an answer that is so self-evident that I almost insult your intelligence by referring to it. But I give you a three-fold answer.

The first answer is: Some of you can respond to God's call and go. I speak particularly to the young people. May you live close enough in fellowship with God that you can hear His voice speaking to you through the Word of God. Prepare your heart and life for such a ministry.

Some of us remember with great moving of heart the story that comes to us from Scotland, the volunteering of the missionary servant of God that stirs our hearts by all that he did under God, Alexander Duff. You recall the story? There was a missionary meeting in the church, and the people's hearts were stirred and moved, and a special offering was received for the taking of the Gospel to the ends of the earth. People with tears in their eyes, choked with emotion as well as sobered by the information that had come to them to make them sense their responsibility, began to give, and to give lavishly for their work of God. Little Alexander Duff, just a boy ten years of age or so, was seated in the pew, his own heart strangely moved and warmed by God. But he had nothing to give. So after that the plate had been passed from pew to pew, and all the offerings had been received, as the ushers were standing in the rear of the church, Alexander Duff got up from the pew where he was and ran to the back of the church and looked full into the face of the usher and said, "Sir, put the plate low." The usher, wondering just what was involved, did just as the boy instructed and put the plate on the floor. The boy stood on the plate and by that act of consecration said, "Oh God, I give myself in the offering." And the boy never wavered. He went as God's missionary servant.

Some of you, if you are living close enough to God, will hear His voice. You will bless the day that you made the decision to be what God wants you to be, an ambassador to those in the chains of the slavery of sin. You can go.

There is something else you can do. You can give. Oh, I tell you, when once you recognize that souls outside of Christ are lost, that you have an indebtedness, then you have a responsibility as before God to share with others the message that you have. It is going to loosen the strings of your purse, and you are going to begin to give as you have never given: giving liberally, giving joyously, giving gladheartedly. Oh, may I say to you, dare to believe God! Dare to get into the on-march of the purpose of God in reaching a world without the Saviour. Dare to test God! I would say to you, dare even to increase the pledge that already you have made. I want to tell you from personal experience, I want to tell you from experience as a pastor, God will more than compensate. I am not speaking materially; I am not speaking financially — God will take care of you that way, I am sure — I am speaking of the joy of your soul as you begin to be brought up into the very purposes of God, the thing that God has put us here to do. Dare to trust Him. Dare to give.

And the third thing — and I leave it to the last, not because it is unimportant, but because it is the most important — that is, you can pray. No one who has ever been on a foreign mission field fails to recognize the tremendous importance of a ministry of prayer on behalf of those who are serving God in other lands. It seems as though the forces of the enemy and the oppression of the devil is on every side; and I remind you that God has ordained to bless as we pray. I trust that the naming of a missionary glibly in prayer before you tumble into bed has long since been insufficient for you. God help you to have your prayer list, and daily to remember them by name; to pray for them, for they are in the vortex of the battle. We stand with them as we pray and as we meet together at the Throne of Grace.

In my judgment — you may disagree with me if you desire — but in my judgment, the Church at home is only as strong as is its missionary outlook. God loves to bless those who are in the on-march of what He is doing; and there are other sheep that Christ must reach. There are lost souls that Christ must win. And you may have a share, and I may have a share in that operation of God.

God help us to do what He wants us to do; so that we shall not be ashamed, when we give our account to Him.

III

WHERE SHALL WE WORK?
Oswald J. Smith

In Proverbs 24:11,12 we find these words, "If thou forbear to deliver them that are drawn unto death, and those that are ready to be slain; If thou sayest, Behold, we knew it not; doth not he that pondereth the heart consider it? and he that keepeth thy soul, doth not he know it? and shall not he render to every man according to his works?"

"If thou forbear." If we refuse to go to the help of those in need. If we claim ignorance. What about it? God says we will be judged according to our works. There can be no excuse. If souls are perishing, we must do what we can to rescue them.

I. Only Two Groups

If there were two companies of people before me, one that had not eaten for a week and the other having had three meals a day, to which company would I offer food? To those who had eaten, or to those who had not? The answer is obvious. Can I then give my money for work in the homeland, or ought I to give it for the sending of missionaries to those who have never heard? Some day God will demand an accounting. Why should we force the Gospel upon those who have rejected it, when there are still millions who have never even heard it?

There are just two groups in this world of ours today — those who have heard the Gospel and those who have not; those who

Oswald J. Smith is pastor of the People's Church, Toronto, Ontario, Canada. Probably few men in the history of the church have been as influential in the promotion of missions as has this man in his own church and in scores of others. The People's Church shares in the support of 360 missionaries and their missionary giving exceeds $250,000.00 per year.

can hear and those who cannot. And so far as I am concerned, I am for those who have not. *Untold millions are still untold.*

When I think of gospel radio programs, the tens of thousands of churches, the millions of tracts, the great evangelistic campaigns, and the multitudes of Christian organizations and workers here in the homeland, and then compare it with the almost complete absence of such endeavors among the tribes and peoples still untold, my whole soul revolts within me at the shame of it, the unfairness and injustice.

In a certain city a missionary turned on the radio and got a gospel program. He turned the dial and got another. Again he turned it and got a third. There were over forty religious broadcasts on the air that day. Think of it — the same Gospel to the same people at the same time! What overlapping! And all supported by God's money, money that might have been used to broadcast the message in a foreign land. Is it fair? Is it right? What must God think of us?

There is a popular song today called "It Is No Secret," and it says, "It is no secret what God can do." But it is. To countless millions it is still a secret. They do not know what God can do. They do not know because they have not been told.

"Faith cometh by hearing, and hearing by the word of God." But "how shall they hear without a preacher" — or without a missionary? "And how shall they preach except they be sent?" (Romans 10:17,14,15). There is no other way. How many have you sent? What have you done? Do you give all your money here at home where there is so much overlapping, or are you sending out substitutes to the regions beyond? Are you going to labor here where laborers are treading on each other's toes, or are you going to labor out there where you will have no competition? When a pulpit here became vacant two hundred pastors tried to get it. Out there each one could have had a whole tribe to himself.

Well now, what are we going to do about it? There is just one question that we need ask: "Have they heard or have they not?" "Can they hear or can they not?" If they have, then let us think twice before giving more of our money. If they have not, and cannot, then we have a challenge to meet, a work to do, and a job to complete.

I say again, there are only two groups — those who have heard and those who have not, and you must identify yourself with one or the other. *WHICH IS IT TO BE?* Why should anyone hear the Gospel twice before everyone has heard it once?

II. WE MUST EVANGELIZE OUR GENERATION

This generation can only reach this generation. This generation cannot reach the last generation because the heathen of the last generation are all dead and gone. The Christians of the last generation were responsible for the heathen of the last generation. This generation cannot reach the next generation because when the heathen of the next generation will have been born, the Christians of this generation will have died. The only generation that we can reach is our own generation and unless we evangelize our generation, it will never be evangelized.

In our Canadian Northwest, we have great harvest fields. Every autumn special trains, loaded with harvesters, are rushed to these fields. Why the haste? Why the hurry? Why not take our time? Why not do it later? Why must it be done now? Because it is now or never. The harvest will not wait. There may be another, but this harvest will be lost, and lost forever. It must be garnered within the limits of a single harvest season or it will perish. Hence the haste. So it is with the Lord's harvest. There may be those who will reach a future generation, but this generation will be lost and will perish unevangelized. Hence, the urgency.

Some one generation must complete the evangelization of the world. Why not our generation? Why leave it to another? The last generation did not do it, and the next may not. It must be completed, I say, within the limits of a single generation. Why not within the limits of our own? We can do it if we will.

III. Can It Be Done?

But, you say, if it has already taken nearly two thousand years to evangelize thirty-five per cent of the human race, how can the remaining sixty-five per cent be evangelized within the next few years? Will it not take another two thousand years to complete the task? I think not. With our speed-up methods of evangelization, it can be done in this generation. With our modern inventions it is possible.

Today we are using radio broadcasting stations and we are placing them in strategic centers throughout the world. Over these stations we will be able to broadcast the Gospel in the languages of the people to multiplied thousands and reach more in a single hour than we formerly could in years.

We have public address systems. I think of a missionary in North Africa who placed a loud speaker on top of his roof garden and from it broadcast the Gospel to the whole town. Personally, he never could have penetrated behind the closed doors where the Mohammedan women were kept in confinement; nor could he have compelled the Moslem men to listen. But his message from the roof-top pierced the walls and doors of all the houses and reached everywhere in the entire town. That method will evangelize anywhere, and thus speed up the getting out of the Gospel.

We are using transcriptions today, thousands of them. They are made by the natives themselves and even though the language has never been reduced to writing and the missionary does not know a word of it, these transcriptions can be played in the most remote villages and hundreds of eager listeners will crowd around to hear the singing and the messages in their own native tongue. The record says the same thing over and over again, until the people know it by heart. They cannot argue with it. All they can do is to hear it and then accept or reject the message.

Planes are being used today, and in many mountainous districts, where it used to take the missionary six weeks to reach the field of service, it now takes him two hours, and when he arrives he is fresh and ready for work. The long, tiresome trip through forests, mountains and valleys is a thing of the past on many fields. He can travel from the homeland to the foreign field in a few hours and arrive ready for work. If he is sick, he can be brought home quickly for an emergency operation. Planes are solving many of the problems of the missionary.

With all these methods for the getting out of the Gospel, it should be quite possible to complete the evangelization of the world within the limits of our own generation, even though there are still more than a thousand tribes to be evangelized. It is the urgency of the task that must move us to action. Had the Church realized just how urgent it is, the world would have been evangelized long, long ago.

IV. THREE DIFFERENT GROUPS

I would like to challenge three different groups. First of all, the senders, then the pray-ers, and last but not least, the go-ers. All three are necessary.

Someone must send: money is necessary. There are those who will have to hold the ropes at home. And if you, my friend, cannot go, then perhaps God wants you to be a sender and to see that another goes in your place. Your part is to earn money and make it possible for someone else to go. And remember, you will share equally in the reward.

Then there are the pray-ers. It may be that you cannot earn money and that you only have sufficient for your own needs. You may never be able to send another; but you can be a pray-er. You can spend a little time in Africa, and India, and China, each day. You can get a list of missionaries and pray for them. That may be your responsibility, and if it is, woe betide you if you shirk it. You, too, may win a reward by faithfully praying for those who have gone; thus you can have a share in their work.

Then, of course, there are the go-ers, and if you are healthy and strong, if you have or can get the necessary training, and if you are prepared, you can go. The urge will come upon you as you pray about your life's work and you will soon know if God is calling. I challenge you to the greatest work in the world. I appeal to you to go if you can. There is nothing like it. The missionaries are God's aristocrats. They are the aristocracy of the church. You will be associating with the finest people on earth.

V. How to Know God's Will

How will you know God's will? Let me tell you. Start now praying about your life's work. Pray every day. Set aside time for prayer and cry out, "Lord, what wilt Thou have me to do?" Then, as you pray, read missionary biography—Brainerd, Singh, Livingstone, Carey, Moffet, MacKay, Judson, Paton, Slessor, Chalmers, Morrison, Duff, Martyn, Williams, Taylor, Geddie. Read two or three chapters each day. That will put you into the atmosphere of missions. Then, as you read and pray, not forgetting, of course, God's Word, there will come to your heart a conviction, an urge that God wants you to serve Him in some foreign land. If not, the burden will lift. That urge is the voice of the Spirit. Heed it, and you will never go astray.

When you are sure of God's will, do not let Satan turn you aside. He will if he can. Your own friends and loved ones may become your greatest stumbling blocks. Be on your guard. Many a girl who has been called has married a man who was not going, and vice-versa, with the result that God's plan has been missed. Listen, young people, you have no right even to keep company with anyone except someone who is traveling in your direction. Do that and you will never make a mistake. God has already chosen your life partner for you and His choice is ever so much better than yours. Don't let Satan turn you aside.

When Mary Slessor first went to Africa, she found herself among cannibals. Human sacrifices were offered. When a chief died, heads were cut off, wives buried alive or killed and eaten. Hands were dipped in boiling oil.

Only the Gospel has changed all this. But, thank God, it has. And oh, what Christians these Africans make! Alexander Mackay tells of the three boys who died for Christ. Their ages were twelve to fifteen. The eldest stepped forward singing a gospel hymn. They cut off his arms, and then threw him into the fire and burned him alive. They did the same with the second. Then came the turn of the youngest, only twelve. "Please don't cut off my arms," he pleaded. "I will not struggle. Just throw me into the fire." What heroes!

In the South Sea Islands there is a tablet. It was erected to the memory of John Geddes, and this is the inscription on it: "When he landed in 1848 there were no Christians here, and when he left in 1872 there were no heathen." Such is the power of the Gospel.

The problem is still one of laborers. In China there are vast harvest fields and they have to be reaped by hand; yet they are always reaped. Why? Because every man, woman, boy and girl, able to carry a sickle, goes to work; hence, there are laborers in abundance.

Our Lord recognized that problem. He said, "The harvest is plenteous but the labourers are few. Pray ye therefore the Lord of the harvest, that he will send forth labourers into His harvest" (Matthew 9:37,38). If we had a sufficient number of laborers, the job could be done, but we have always been short-handed. Today, with our increased population, the laborers are as few, in comparison, as they were in the days of Jesus. That is why we are continually appealing to young men and women to volunteer for missionary service. We must get more laborers.

Dr. Alexander Duff, that great veteran missionary to India, returned to Scotland to die. As he stood before the General Assembly of the Presbyterian Church, he made his appeal, but there was no response. In the midst of the appeal, he fainted and was carried off the platform. The doctor bent over him and examined his heart. Presently he opened his eyes. "Where am I?" he cried. "Where am I?"

"Lie still," said the doctor. "Your heart is very weak."

"But," exlaimed the old warrior, "I must finish my appeal. Take me back. Take me back. I haven't finished my appeal yet."

"Lie still," said the doctor again, "you are too weak to go back."

But the aged missionary struggled to his feet, his determination overcoming his weakness, and with the doctor on one side and the moderator on the other side, the old white-haired warrior was led again to the platform, and, as he mounted the pulpit steps, the entire Assembly rose to do him honor. Then he continued his appeal.

"When Queen Victoria calls for volunteers for India," he exclaimed, "hundreds of young men respond; but when King Jesus calls, no one goes." Then he paused. Again he spoke. "Is it true," he asked, "that Scotland has no more sons to give for India?" Again he paused. "Very well," he concluded, "if Scotland has no more young men to send to India, then, old and decrepit though I am, I will go back, and even though I cannot preach, I can lie down on the shores of the Ganges and die, in order to let the people of India know that there is at least one man in Scotland who cares enough for their souls to give his life for them."

In a moment young men, all over the assembly, sprang to their feet, crying out, "I'll go! I'll go! I'll go!" And after the famous missionary had passed on, many of those same young men found their way to India, there to invest their lives as missionaries, as a result of the appeal God had made through Dr. Duff.

My friend, will you go? Has God spoken to you? Have you heard His call? Will you not answer, "Lord, here am I, send me"? And if you cannot go, will you send a substitute? It is for you to decide.

Why should anyone hear the Gospel twice before everyone has heard it once?

IV

WHY EVANGELIZE THE HEATHEN?
G. Christian Weiss

To a missionary, the words of the Lord Jesus in Mark 16:15 are as familiar as John 3:16 to the evangelist. But, though these words are exceedingly familiar to us, they may not be so familiar to some others. Let us look at this Scripture, beginning at verse 9:

Now when Jesus was risen early the first day of the week, he appeared first to Mary Magdalene, out of whom he had cast seven devils. And she went and told them that had been with him, as they mourned and wept. And they, when they had heard that he was alive, and had been seen of her, believed not. After that he appeared in another form unto two of them, as they walked, and went into the country. And they went and told it unto the residue: neither believed they them. Afterward he appeared unto the eleven as they sat at meat, and upbraided them with their unbelief and hardness of heart, because they believed not them which had seen him after he was risen. And he said unto them, Go ye into all the world, and preach the gospel to every creature.

"Go ye into all the world," Christ said, "And preach the gospel to every creature." I would like to discuss the answer to the question, *"Why seek to evangelize the heathen?"* People ask, "Why bother the heathen?" "Why persuade them to give up *their* religion and accept *our* religion?" "Why give so much

---

G. Christian Weiss was formerly General Director of the Gospel Missionary Union and now is Director of Missions with the Back to the Bible Broadcast Radio Program which supports a large number of missionaries through its ministry.

money to foreign missions?" "Why send all these young people to other countries to make Christians out of the heathen?" Why? Why? Why?

I

First of all, in answer to this question, let me say,

We Must Evangelize the Heathen Because The Lord Jesus Christ Commanded Us to Do So

He said it plainly; there is no uncertainty regarding the words He used in the Great Commission: "Go ye into all the world and preach the gospel to every creature." This is our Saviour's imperative word to His followers, to the Christian Church. It is a command, not merely a request, or a suggestion, but a positive command, coming from the lips of Christ our Lord. "Go ye," He said to His disciples, "into all the world, and preach the gospel to every creature." Are you a Christian today? Are you a follower of the Lord Jesus Christ? Are you one of those who has become a child of God through faith in Him? Do you answer in the affirmative and yet presume to say that you do not believe in evangelizing the heathen? My friend, this is impossible! To say you are a Christian, but that you do not believe in sending the Gospel to the heathen nations, is an utterly impossible position, for it is the equivalent of saying, "I believe on the Lord Jesus, I love Him, and am following Him, but I don't believe we should do what He told us to do." You see, He has plainly told us to go into all the world and preach the Gospel to every creature, so if you say you are a Christian, but you do not believe in missions, you are putting yourself in an obviously impossible position. It is not possible to be a genuine Christian and at the same time disbelieve doing what the Lord Jesus commanded us, that is, to take the Gospel into all the world and to every creature.

Has that commission ever been carried out? Has that task ever been completed? Has the Gospel gone into all the world? Has it been proclaimed to every human being? Of course it hasn't. There has not been a generation since Jesus gave this command, when the whole world has been evangelized. There has never been a single generation from the time of Christ until now, when an entire generation of men knew the story of Jesus Christ and of His gospel. Hence the commission still stands.

II

The second reason we must evangelize the heathen is that

The Heathen Need the Gospel
If They Are to Be Saved

Now there are people who think the heathen can be saved without the Gospel. Most believers seem to understand that in a Bible-enlightened country like our own, a person must be born-again to become a Christian, but at the same time they somehow think people who have not heard the Gospel and who do not know anything about Christ can be saved without the Gospel. But, I say to you, it is impossible for anyone, anywhere, to be saved without being born-again. Jesus said, "Except *a man be born again he cannot see* the kingdom of God." If these words be true they include people from far-away dark Africa and all the rest of the world. If a man anywhere could be saved without being born again these words of the Lord Jesus would be rendered meaningless. But when He said, "Except a man be born again, he cannot see the kingdom of God," He meant exactly that.

The apostle Paul was sent to the heathen "to open their eyes, to turn them from darkness to light, and from the power of Satan unto God, that they might receive the forgiveness of sins" (Acts 26:18). Obviously if Paul was sent to the heathen to open their eyes, that meant that they were held under the power of Satan. That they might receive the forgiveness of sins, means that up until that time they *could not* receive such forgiveness.

In the second chapter of the book of Ephesians, verse 12, the apostle Paul writes, "That at that time (i.e. when they were still in their days of heathenism) ye were without Christ, being aliens from the commonwealth of Israel, and strangers from the covenants of promise, having no hope, and without God in the world." The Word of God here says plainly and explicitly that those who do not know Christ are without God and that they are without hope.

We must evangelize the heathen because no man can be saved without coming to know about Jesus Christ. "Whosoever shall call upon the name of the Lord shall be saved" — because Christ died for all men. "How then, shall they call upon Him in whom they have not believed? and how shall they believe in him of whom they have not heard? and how shall they hear without a preacher?" *We have the remedy* for the souls of men. We have the message of eternal life. We have that which can solve the needs and the problems of the hearts of heathen men and women, both in this life and in eternity. Will we give it to them or will we continue to withhold it?

III

A third reason for the evangelization of the world is that

Self-Interest Demands It

The religion of Islam is growing by leaps and bounds throughout the Eastern Hemisphere and is developing even right in our own land. Where we are failing to get the Gospel to certain heathen people, heathen religions are being planted right at our doorsteps at home. I say, therefore, self-interest demands that we take the Gospel to the heathen.

Communism today is sweeping over the world. Consider what a large portion of the world's population already is behind its iron curtain; and Communism is aggressively at work in most of the heathen countries. Where we are failing to get the Gospel to the heathen the emissaries of this godless religion are giving them the propaganda of Communism. If we are to save certain large portions of the earth from its control, we must get the message of Christ to those people and into their hearts.

For example, in the great country of Japan where the doors have been open so wide to the Gospel, those doors, in a sense, have been equally open wide to Communism, and its devotees have been making full use of the opportunity. They have been exerting more effort to get the doctrines of Communism into the minds and hearts of the Japanese people than we Christians have toward getting the message of Christ to them. That same truth applies to multitudes today in other parts of the Orient — in fact, all over the world, including Latin America. If we sit idly by and let these multitudes be won over to Communism, instead of winning them to Christ, we are going to suffer, and suffer severely for it.

The surest hope now for saving Europe from Communism is Christian revival, a renewal of the Gospel of the Lord Jesus Christ in these countries. Even the statesmen recognize this. In many of these countries, it is "Christ or Communism." Self-interest, then, if no other reason, demands that we should evangelize the world. It is the only force that can stop the tremendous growth of the Terrible Monster.

IV

A fourth reason why we must evangelize the world is to

Hasten the Return of the Lord Jesus Christ

In the first chapter of the book of Acts the disciples asked Jesus, "Lord, will you at this time restore the kingdom to Israel?" He answered, in effect, "The time and the season when I shall set up the kingdom on earth is not for you to know; The Father will do that in His own good time. But there is something else for you to do. You tarry in Jerusalem until the Spirit comes, and when He comes, you start right in here and be witnesses unto me in Jerusalem, Judaea and Samaria, and on out into all nations until you have gone to the uttermost part of the earth, in order that through the preaching of this gospel, men and women might believe on me and by so doing become children of God." Then in chapter 15 of Acts we have the record of the first council meeting in the early church, considering whether or not the converts from among the heathen would have to be circumcised. James, who acted as chairman, says in verse 14, "Simeon hath declared how God at the first did visit the Gentiles, to take out of them a people for his name. And to this agree the words of the prophets; as it is written. After this I will return, and will build again the tabernacle of David, which is fallen down; and I will build again the ruins thereof, and I will set it up:"

Notice the statement that God, following the crucifixion of Jesus Christ, would first visit the nations (all nations, the heathen) and take out from them a people for His name, that is to say, the church, the body of Christ. *"After this,"* after the Gospel has gone to all the heathen nations, and after God has taken out from among these nations a people for His name, then Jesus will return and will build again the tabernacle of David which is fallen down. So if we will hasten with this work of world evangelism, if we hasten with the Gospel to the hundreds of unreached tribes, so that the Spirit of God through the living Word can gather out of every kindred, tongue, people and nation, those who are to constitute the body of Christ, we shall thus hasten the return of the Lord. Jesus will not come until His body has been made complete, and the Scriptures declare very plainly that His body (the Church) is to be made up of every kindred, and tongue, and people, and nation. Hence, I believe that we as Christians may hasten or delay the coming of our Lord by the way we respond to the task of giving the Gospel to the heathen.

My esteemed friend, Oswald J. Smith, well known over the Christian world as a great missionary pastor, has for years been veritably obsessed with the passion to get the Gospel to the unreached tribes, that the body of Christ may be completed, and that he might thus have a part in the hastening of the return of the Lord. Ah yes, we as Christians *can hasten* the bringing back of the King.

V

A fifth reason why we must evangelize the world is

Because of the Reward That Is in Store

Oh, the reward that comes to the heart of each missionary! I can speak here as from experience and can tell you something of the *joy of preaching the Gospel to men and women who previously were in heathen darkness,* and the joy of seeing some of them, as they believed on the Lord Jesus Christ, turn from darkness to light, from the power of Satan to God to become brothers and sisters with us in the faith of the Lord Jesus Christ. Not only does the missionary have that inward reward here and now in this life, but there is a greater reward waiting for him in glory. Those who give are rewarded as well as those who go to the field.

Missionary funds have begun to lag. This is being felt in many circles and in many societies. More candidates are ready to go than there are funds available to send. Others are sorely in need of important equipment that would greatly expand their efforts and increase their efficiency. There is a desperate need in most of the foreign fields for multiplied quantities of Christian literature — printed matter. The needs are not being met in any degree of true adequacy. This is tragic. With the possibility of many doors closing or already closed, it is woeful that the open doors cannot be efficiently entered because of the lack of funds.

Perhaps you or your church should be supporting a missionary of your own. Mission boards will gladly assign you one. In many fields, a missionary may be fully supported for approximately one hundred dollars per month. The Back to the Bible Broadcast, Lincoln, Nebraska, will be delighted to supply you with the name of a missionary under a good reliable board who needs support. It is the privilege of any person thus supporting a missionary, to correspond directly with that missionary, and this in itself is a real reward of joy and blessing. If you cannot fully support a missionary yourself, perhaps you can get a Christian friend or relative to join you in doing it.

The words of Jesus, pertaining to Christian reward, as found in John 4:36 are: "And he that reapeth receiveth wages, and gathereth fruit unto life eternal: that both he that soweth and he that reapeth may rejoice together."

Here, then, are some of the reasons why we must evangelize the unevangelized world. God help us to do it.

V

LABOR TROUBLE
Lee Roberson

And Jesus went about all the cities and villages, teaching in their synagogues, and preaching the gospel of the kingdom, and healing every sickness and every disease among the people.

But when he saw the multitudes, he was moved with compassion on them, because they fainted, and were scattered abroad, as sheep having no shepherd. Then saith he unto his disciples, The harvest truly is plenteous, but the labourers are few. Pray ye therefore the Lord of the harvest, that he will send forth labourers into his harvest (Matthew 9:35-38).

Labor trouble is an old trouble. One of the first accounts of labor trouble is given in the first book of the Bible. It occurred between the herdmen of Abram's cattle and the herdmen of Lot's cattle.

"And there was a strife between the herdmen of Abram's cattle and the herdmen of Lot's cattle: and the Canaanite and the Perizzite dwelled then in the land" (Genesis 13:7).

This trouble was quickly settled by the unselfishness of one man, Abraham. Labor trouble will always be settled by the unselfishness of men — it is the only way.

There was labor trouble in Egypt. The Israelites were made to work for the Egyptians. We read, "And the Egyptians made the children of Israel to serve with rigor: And they made their lives bitter with hard bondage in mortar and in brick, and in all

Lee Roberson is President of the Tennessee Temple Schools, Chattanooga, Tenn. Scores of young people from the Bible School and College have gone forth as missionaries. In the church of which he is pastor, Highland Park Baptist Church, Chattanooga, he has established a strong missionary church, supporting well over 100 missionaries under many missionary societies. He is constantly encouraging churches to begin missionary conferences.

manner of service in the field: All their service, wherein they made them serve, was with rigour" (Exodus 1:13,14).

There was labor trouble in Nehemiah's day. When he returned to rebuild the walls of Jerusalem, some of the residents of the country opposed and ridiculed the project. Nehemiah and his people went forward with the work at great cost and effort.

There was labor trouble in Paul's day. He gave this exhortation to the people in Thessalonica.

"For even when we were with you, this we commanded you, that if any would not work, neither should he eat. For we hear that there are some which walk among you disorderly, working not at all, but are busybodies. Now them that are such we command and exhort by our Lord Jesus Christ, that with quietness they work, and eat their own bread" (II Thessalonians 3:10-12).

James, in his book, recognized labor trouble in his day. In Chapter 5 he gives sharp words to the rich and to those who would defraud the laborer of his hire.

There is labor trouble today all over the world. It is here in America, it is in foreign countries. There is great dissatisfaction, both among employers and employees. This will continue throughout this age. Why? Because of sin. Men are selfish, covetous, lazy, envious and thoughtless. There can be only one solution to the labor problem, and that is the Lord Jesus Christ in the hearts of men.

There was also labor trouble in the day of our Lord. This labor trouble was of a very special kind. It is indicated to us in Matthew 9:3-38. Observe four things in this portion of Scripture.

1. Christ's vision. "But when he saw the multitudes. . ." The eyes of our Lord were always open to see the needs of people.

2. Christ's compassion. "He was moved with compassion on them because they fainted, and were scattered abroad as sheep having no shepherd." When the eyes of the Master beheld men, His heart was moved to do something for them.

3. Christ's appraisal. He looked upon the multitudes, He was moved with compassion, and then He said, "The harvest truly is plenteous, but the labourers are few."

4. Christ's remedy. "Pray ye therefore the Lord of the harvest, that he will send forth labourers into his harvest." It is apparent that one of our great needs is for more prayer for people to labor for the Lord.

I would like to call your attention to three things:

I. The Task

Labor trouble implies work. Is there a task for every Christian? Is there a work to be done? Is this task teaching, preaching, singing? Does it belong to just a few, or does it belong to everyone?

The answer is plain. There is a job for every child of God. That job is witnessing. We are saved to serve and that service is witnessing and winning souls.

Though the Christian may be called upon to do a number of things, the end of every task is the winning of the lost. Someone tells of the minister who called his leaders together and said that he was going to resign his ministry at the church because he had seen no one saved for a considerable period. They begged him to stay, and pointed out how edified they were by his preaching.

"Edified for what?" he asked. Turning to one leader, he asked him if he had ever led a soul to Christ. The answer was no. The question was put to the next and the next with the same result. Finally, the minister got all of the members of the meeting to promise that they would also resign with him if within a short period they personally led no one to Christ. The end of the story is that a revival broke out and many were won within a short period of time.

Every agency and every organization of the church should be directed toward one end — the winning of the lost. Whether we preach, sing, teach, preside, or whatever our task may be, it should be for the purpose that men receive the message of Christ and be saved.

Here is the task: Andrew came to Jesus and was saved. The Scriptures tell us that he went out and found his own brother, Simon, and brought him to Jesus. Andrew put his hand to the task at once and did the very thing that God had saved him to do. He found his own brother, Simon, and testified to him and then brought him to Christ.

Here is the task: Four men were concerned about a poor para-lytic. They bore him to Jesus, and Jesus saved his soul and healed his body. These four men were applying themselves to the task of bringing others to Christ.

Here it is: Philip was a deacon in the church in Jerusalem. As a deacon, he felt called upon to apply himself to the main task. He went to Samaria and preached the Gospel. Souls were saved and a mighty work was done. He was called away from this revival to go into the desert and there he led the Ethiopian eunuch to Christ. He was applying himself to the task as given by the Lord.

Here it is again: Paul and Silas, two missionaries, went to the town of Philippi. They began at once their work of witnessing. It was not long until there were converts: first Lydia, then the jailor, and his household, and others.

Have you been applying yourself to the task? Excuses will not avail. God is asking for faithfulness.

We have a divine task. It is given to us by our Lord. It was not committed unto angels, but unto us, the children of God.

We have an urgent task. There is no time for delay, for men are passing out into eternity without knowing Christ.

We have a demanding task. It calls for the best that every person can give.

We have an eternal task. By this, I mean that when we en-gage in this work, the results will tell for eternity. Buildings may be built, bridges may be constructed, highways may be made, but they will all disappear. But the work of witnessing will abide forever.

Look now to the fields white unto harvest. Is your heart not stirred by the great multitudes without our Saviour? Think of the millions who have never heard of Christ even once. Think of the need among the various nationalities in our nation. Think of a town of 125,000 people with hardly a single representative of evangelical Christianity.

The fields are white unto harvest. May we look upon them. May we pray. May we give, and may we go.

II. The Trouble

Christ said, "We have labor trouble" — "The harvest is plenteous, but the laborers are few." This seems strange when we consider the following:

We have labor trouble with God calling men. Yes, the Lord is calling each one of you, even as Jesus called Peter, James and John, Matthew and others. God is calling you, even as He called Samuel and Gideon and Elijah. Perhaps you are saying, "Where is the call?" It is written down in God's Word. To every child of God, the command is given, "Go ye."

We have labor trouble with God paying. Our Heavenly Father pays the best of wages. We are rewarded here and hereafter. Christ said to His disciples, "Everyone that hath forsaken houses, or brethren, or sisters, or father, or mother, or wife, or children, or lands, for my name's sake, shall receive an hundred fold, and shall inherit everlasting life" (Matthew 19:29).

Think of the joy that God gives to us as we labor for Him on this earth. Think of the blessings of peace and joy which are ours because of Christ in our hearts. Think of His presence through every hour and every difficulty. What wonderful wages we receive, and yet we will be receiving blessings for eternity.

We have labor trouble with God supplying the strength. No man is asked to serve God in his own strength. The Lord says that He will give power unto us. He promises to supply all of our needs through Christ Jesus. Paul said, "I can do all things through Christ which strengtheneth me." When you are weary, He gives encouragement. When you are weak, He gives you power. This is what Isaiah said about it:

"He giveth power to the faint; and to them that have no might he increaseth strength. Even the youths shall faint and be weary, and the young men shall utterly fall: But they that wait upon the Lord shall renew their strength; they shall mount up with wings as eagles; they shall run, and not be weary; and they shall walk, and not faint" (Isaiah 40:29-31).

Again, we have labor troubles with Christ as a co-worker. "For we are laborers together with God; ye are God's husbandry, ye are God's building" (I Corinthians 3:9). What a privilege to labor with the Lord at your side. So often at public work, men are cast into the midst of unfavorable working companions, but not so with those who labor for Christ. He is our helper.

In spite of all that seems good, we have labor trouble. First, there is the trouble of quantity. Jesus said, "The labourers are few." Too few men and women to do the job! Too few who care, who are willing to pay the price for real service. It would seem that with all the people who are volunteering for the mission fields, that we would have an over-abundance. But this is far from being the case. There is a desperate need for missionaries around the world. There is a dearth of pastors and evangelists in certain parts of the country. The harvest is ready, but there are no laborers.

Not only is there trouble in quantity, but there is trouble in quality. Many volunteer to serve, but through laziness, confusion, procrastination and lack of separation, they do not make good workers.

There are many who have said, "Yes, Lord, I am going to be a witness for Thee," but they are still procrastinating. It may be that timidity is holding some back. Whatever it may be, there is a need of quality among the workers for Christ.

Therefore, there is serious labor trouble because of the lack of workers; willing workers who will lay down their lives for Christ. Again, there is a need for faithful workers who will carry on to the end of the way, and be able to say with the apostle Paul, "I have fought a good fight, I have finished the course, I have kept the faith."

Our labor trouble can be dispelled by three things. First, by realization of the importance of the task. A man will volunteer for a life and death job. He will stay with the work when he realizes that it is of tremendous importance. There is no labor trouble when men join together to rescue another from drowning. There was no labor trouble when hundreds of men and women banded together to rescue the little girl from the old well. Labor troubles will be solved when men realize that it is God who calls and commissions, and that without obedience souls will perish forever.

Again, this work requires dedication. There must be a whole-hearted consecration of our all unto Christ. Withholding the smallest part of our time or talents will cause a disruption in the work and failure to some part of it. Dedication to the task of getting the Gospel to men will solve the trouble.

Thirdly, there must be concentration. If the quality of the work is to be satisfactory, then the Christian workers must say, "This one thing I do."

III. The Time

What is the task? Witnessing. What is the trouble? Too few and too poor in quality.

What is the time? It is now. There is no time for delay. Our lives are passing, our energies fail, our opportunities disappear. Sinners are dying. The time for work is now.

It is an interesting story given us in John 4. We read of Christ talking to the woman at the well in Samaria. His disciples went into a nearby place to buy food. Jesus dealt tenderly and yet positively with the sinful woman. She had accepted Him as Saviour and went away to tell others about Him. When the disciples of Jesus returned, they urged Him to eat, but Christ said, "I have meat to eat that ye know not of." The disciples were confused and said, "Hath any man brought him ought to eat?" Christ made answer, "My meat is to do the will of him that sent me and to finish his work."

And so, our Lord tells us of the time for work. "Say not ye, There is yet four months and then cometh harvest. Behold,

I say unto you, Lift up your eyes and look on the fields, for they are white already to harvest."

O Christian, now is the time! Your delays are dangerous and inexcusable. The fields are white and ready for harvest. Do not make excuses. Do not blame the hardness of men's hearts. Do not say that you are too busy to take part in this work. Quit being a problem and begin to be a worker.

The story is told of a rich English merchant to whom the queen gave a commission of importance. He hesitated to undertake it, saying, "Please, your majesty, if I obey your command, what will become of these affairs of mine?"

The queen answered, "Leave those things to me. When you are employed in my service, I will take charge of your business."

So it will be with everyone of us. If we put the work of our Saviour first, He will take care of our affairs.

To the churches of Asia Minor, the Lord said, "I know thy works." To the church at Ephesus, the Lord said, "I have somewhat against thee, because thou hast left thy first love." What is the first love of a Christian? It is to tell someone else about Jesus.

Christ is looking at you today and saying, "I know thy works." Many of us need to hang our heads in shame as we come to the consciousness of how the Lord knows us.

The fields are white unto harvest. He commands us to go. It is obey or disobey.

The needs of men are all around us. Do we look upon the multitudes and have compassion as did Jesus?

The common gratitude of a man's heart should compel him to go. Do you love the Lord? Are you grateful for the salvation which is yours? Go into the harvest fields. Do the work which the Lord has commanded you to do. Christian, God calls you. God needs you. And God wants you. I lay the challenge squarely before you — will you accept the task? Now is the time!

VI

THE MAKING OF A MISSIONARY WARRIOR
Elmer V. Thompson

*For though I be free from all men yet have I made myself
servant unto all that I might gain the more* (I Corinthians 9:19;
see vss. 20-22, 27).

Effectiveness in foreign missionary work does not rest alone
in the ability to teach the Word or in the fact that one is a Bible-
believing missionary. It is possible to be theologically correct,
highly trained, humanly gifted and zealous as a missionary and
still be relatively useless in the realm of spiritual power. The
fact is, that a considerable portion of the truly evangelical missionaries now on the mission field exert little influence when it
comes to moving for God the people among whom they work.
Thank God, many missionaries are awake to this lack of soul-
challenging power and therefore welcome any light as to its
cause and remedy. Wherein lies the lack?

The Bible passage indicated above goes a long way toward
answering the query. It was written to show the way Paul, the
Apostle, made the Gospel effective among the souls he evangelized. In it, the missionary Apostle discovers several essential
rules for successful missionary activity. Yes, he presents in this
scripture several life procedures which the Gospel missionary in
foreign lands must embrace in order to become a spiritual challenge to the unevangelized.

The key to this ninth chapter of I Corinthians is verse 19.
Here it is: "For though I be free from all men yet have I made

ELMER V. THOMPSON is the founder and Director of the West Indies
Mission, Inc., and has been greatly used of the Lord in missionary ministry
at home.

myself servant unto all that I might gain the more." In the statement of this text, the Apostle reduces the illustrative material he includes in the chapter to three clear permanent life principles. Each of these three parts of this verse presents to our minds one of God's permanent principles for missionary effectiveness. We shall discuss these parts separately and in the order in which they appear in the text.

I. The Principle of Freedom

The first statement in our text is, "Though I be free from all men." Most recent versions of the New Testament put this declaration as, "Though I am free from all men." The words, "Though I am free from all men," are the heart of the statement. By this affirmation the Apostle conveys to us the idea of complete personal emancipation from the fetters and bondages common to men. Power with men finds its basis in a God-given freedom from man. Certainly a slave cannot attract or free others. On the other hand, a free man is a challenge everywhere he goes. It is interesting to note, therefore, that the inspired missionary claims freedom as the foundation upon which his spiritual power and influence were erected.

What does the Apostle mean by the statement, "I am free from all men"? Where does this freeing take place? How does it affect our lives? Going back to verse 1 of the chapter, we note an illustration of the principle of this freedom. "Am I not an apostle, am I not free?" he questions. We all know, that apart from a mighty soul-transforming miracle, the Pharisee Saul would never have been an apostle of the Gospel. Besides this, Paul was divinely appointed. He was free to be what he was because God Himself had liberated his soul and had called him to be a missionary.

Some missionaries are not free under God to be missionaries. They were never freed from self. They never were chosen by God to be missionaries.

Some years ago a junior missionary came to me confessing that he had gone to the field as a result of his wife's desire but without a definite divine call in his own heart. He was finding adjustment to missionary living conditions beyond his power and was experiencing terrific spiritual bondage. He was not free to be a missionary. I have a letter in hand that came to me some time ago. The lady who wrote it served until recently in our work. The dear woman writes: "God is my witness; whatever it takes to make me sincere I accept from Him. My greatest regret is that my husband has been caught in the mesh of my willfulness and that it also affects the lives of countless souls. Is there any hope for me?" Here is a young woman, one of the finest of missionary prospects that this writer has ever met; a sweet, devoted personality, but due to willfulness captivated by an affection that took her out of the will of God, she was not spiritually free to become what God wanted her to be and she is now not at liberty in that which she has become. Oh how important it is to be free before God in life's office!

Paul adds another feature to this discussion of freedom. It relates to the matter of rights and privileges. In verse 4 of chapter 9 (I Corinthians) appears this statement: "Have we not power to eat and drink?" In other words, "Have we not the right to receive our living at the expense of the Church of Jesus Christ?" Verse 5 adds: "Have we not power to lead about a sister, a wife, as well as other apostles?" meaning, "Do we not have the right to be married?" Finally, in verse 6, Paul asks, "Have we not power to forbear working?" That is, "Do we not have the right to devote full time to the gospel ministry and to expect the church to supply our material needs?" The apostle, you see, is writing concerning his material rights and privileges. He had, under God, such rights. All Christians have material rights, but these rights differ the one from the other. There are rights that belong especially to lay Christians. Ministers of the Gospel have particular rights. The same could be said concerning foreign missionaries. These rights are determined by the office one occupies under God. Paul possessed missionary rights and he lived within his rights. He had the right before God to the material privileges he exercised and even more than those he enjoyed.

It is easy to get out of the will of God here. Missionaries easily get over into areas of privilege that do not belong to them. They easily desire and even indulge beyond their God-given rights. A fine young missionary came to me on the field. He was pretty well out of adjustment at the time, but since has become an excellent missionary. This missionary had left a very remunerative employment in the United States and a real possibility for promotion in his trade. He had left it all and had gone to the mission field. On the field he was provided a small house, a small allowance, and was limited in other relations. I remember having a discussion with him one day. He said something like the following: "Mr. Thompson, I did my part when I left my home, when I left my country, when I left my job, when I left my salary and came down here. I think I have a right to live down here just as people do at home." He was wrong. Rights vary with a change of vocation. Missionary rights are not the same as the rights of those assigned by God to the homeland. Missionaries have the right of a living, to be sure, but not the right under God to live as Christians do in the homeland. Such liberty would seriously hamper and damage their example and influence among the peoples to whom they have gone. Missionaries should know Paul's freedom for living happily within the material rights that belong to their calling.

The apostle goes still deeper into this question of freedom. "But I have used none of these things," he testifies in I Corinthians 9:15. What an amazing statement! Paul knew freedom from requiring or exacting his rights. This is freedom on a high level. It is beyond the freedom to be and the freedom to have; it is best expressed as the freedom to forego. Yes, we behold here the freedom by God's grace to forego both the right to be and the right to have. This freedom is seldom exercised today. However, I say with all frankness that apart from this third factor of freedom, missionaries never fully and capably enter into the conflict to which they are called.

I remember talking one time with a dear young woman in Cuba. She was a gifted girl, highly educated, spoke both English and Spanish fluently, and she had capabilities of such a nature that would have made her a tremendous help in our Cuba Bible Institute. I went to this young woman and said, "Miss Matilde, would you consider becoming a teacher with the Cuba Bible Institute? It is a simple life and you know all it involves." She drew back and said, as nearly as I can remember: "Mr. Thompson, I have lived all my life in other people's homes. All my life, I have eaten at the tables of others. I have never had a room that I could call my own. I have never had my own furniture. I am employed with a concern that allows me to serve the Lord Jesus and still accumulate. I want to buy a home for myself. I want to have my own furniture. I want to eat at my own table. Mr. Thompson, I think I have a right to this." I replied, "My dear sister, you are not obligated to accept my offer. You indeed have these rights. I only want to say this. I offer you a higher right. The right to forego that which everyone recognizes as your privilege. I offer you the right to forego all this in the interest of evangelizing the unevangelized of this land, your land, my sister. Think it over." She went home. Three days later Miss Matilde knocked at my door and said, "Mr. Thompson, I have forgotten all about my house." You see, she had foregone her right. She learned a liberty from God that many of God's children have never learned, the right to forego.

There is another freedom here that I must mention. This freedom is not the right to be, nor is it the right to have. It is not the right to forego. Let me call it the right to conform. The great Apostle in writing about it states: "Unto the Jews I became as a Jew that I might gain the Jew; . . . to them that are without the law I became without the law, that I might gain them that are without the law. And to the weak I became as weak that I might gain the weak." There is a principle here of spiritual freedom. Let us term it the release within the soul from self-centeredness and from a life lived to one's own end. Why, even Paul in his day said that he had not but one man who would naturally care for the needs of others. All sought their own. Think of this freedom; freedom to conform, freedom to conform to a lower standard of life than would be normal, freedom to let the other man that lives on the same level have that which is pertinent to that level while I conform to a lower level of life, while I conform to a missionary situation. Too many missionaries on the foreign field find this difficult. It is difficult to conform to a simple life, to the simple life of a simple and primitive people. Yet the whole principle of effective Christianity on the mission field is essentially bound up with this liberation from God. Pray for the young men and women on earth's mission fields that they will know from God the freedom to conform.

II. The Principle of Serving

But Freedom is not all. It is but the basis, the foundation upon which spiritual effectivity is built. Freedom is not enough. One can gloat over his freedom as some do and never get anywhere with it. Paul, in the second statement of our text, shows us the way spiritual freedom should be used. He shows us in this statement the purpose of spiritual freedom. He says, "I have made myself a servant." "What?" you ask. Paul answers, "I have made myself a servant." This is spiritual freedom applied. Its application is in reverse order to material freedom, for in the realm of the natural, freedom signifies the right to serve one's self as one is disposed, whereas in the field of the spiritual, freedom represents the ability or disposition to serve others, as God chooses.

Many Christian workers and missionaries only appreciate four words of this statement. That is, the words "I have made myself." They glory in their attainment, in their accomplishment. "I have made myself a man of importance," say they. "I have made myself a talented preacher, a gifted administrator. I have made myself a missionary who cannot be ignored." These truly take their lives out of the Christian setting as I am applying these four words out of their context. Representatives of the Lord Jesus Christ who thus think of themselves and thus ap-

plaud themselves have yet to learn experimentally the basic
freedom Paul presents in the first statement of our text. One
cannot, like Paul, voluntarily become a servant to the unevangelized heathen until he has been delivered from the applause
and recognition of men and all that is naturally attractive to men.

"I have made myself a servant." Why, this is the very position
we mortals naturally detest! The thing that we naturally work
all our lives to avoid. How absolutely contrary to the natural
way of life is this spiritual pathway! Yes, the path that Paul
marks for the missionary is diametrically opposed to that which
the natural man in him wants and chooses. It is the way of the
Lord Jesus, nevertheless. He came, "not to be ministered unto,
but to minister." Is the servant of the Lord Jesus in this world
to be different from His Lord? No, he is not to be different unless he refuses to make himself a servant.

"I have made myself a servant to all." Paul means by this
statement that he has in respect to his rights, as a missionary of
the church, reduced himself to the position of a slave. The demands a slave may make of his master were the unassuming
requirements Paul laid on the church relative to his services and
his needs as its foreign representative. What may a slave demand
of his master? In respect to the peoples to whom he had gone
as a missionary, Paul means by this declaration that he had made
his own desires, his own likes, subservient, subordinate to their
highest spiritual advantage. He gladly subjected his life to the
varying circumstances prevailing on the different mission fields
where Christ put him. He joyfully adjusted his life to the necessities, to the environment he found among the peoples he served.
Within that which was not contrary to Christ and the Gospel,
he was as elastic as rubber in regard to himself, his convenience
and his desires.

We hear Paul saying in this chapter, "Have we not power
to lead about a sister, a wife, as well as other apostles and as the
brethren of the Lord and Cephas?" And yet Paul had no wife.
We hear Paul saying in this passage, "Have we not power to
eat and to drink?" and yet he makes it plain in this passage

that he and Barnabas often worked with their own hands to pro-
vide the necessities of their bodies. Paul says in this wonderful
chapter, "Unto the Jew I became as a Jew." He subjected himself to the customs, the habits of the Jew for the purpose, as he
puts it, "That I might gain the Jew." He writes concerning the
Gentiles, "To them that are without law, as without law, being
not without law to God but under the law to Christ." Paul,
though a Jew in reality, was not a Jew in custom and habit
among the Gentiles. He accustomed himself to the habits, to the
customs of the Gentiles so far as he could without violating the
law of Christ. He adopted their ways of life as his. He fitted
into their routine and made himself at home among them. This
he did, says he, "That I might gain them that are without law."
Paul triumphantly declares, "I am made all things to all men
that I might by all means save some." This is being a servant
to all.

I remember visiting one of our missionary girls a number of
years ago. This highly talented missionary was working in a
dirty little town among a very backward people. Just before I
visited her this young lady had gone through a trying experience.
A young missionary of our Mission had proposed to this young
woman and then, for some reason, broke off the arrangement.
In that town away from mother and friends our sister faced the
future! I visited her just a few weeks afterward. I remember
asking her, "Are you afraid here?" She replied, "No, Mr.
Thompson, I am not afraid." I then asked, "Do you ever feel
like packing up and leaving this place?" She responded: "Mr.
Thompson, I would not exchange my opportunity here for a
million dollars." That girl, dear readers, is not only free, she is
Christ's servant.

III. THE PRINCIPLE OF GAIN

Now let us turn to the final statement of our text and the
third vital principle for spiritual effectivity presented in I Corinthians 9:19. The clause to be considered is, "That I might gain
the more." These words clearly respond to the question, "Why?"
irrepressibly raised in our minds by the two previous parts — the

two strong statements presented in the first part of our text. We ask, "Why is it so essential that we be free from all men? Why is it so necessary that we take the position of servants with regard to men?" The inspired apostle humbly responds, "That (you) I may gain the more." More "gain" is always an incentive to men. We men are willing to invest more if more "gain" is assured. Now Paul says, "I gain by becoming free from all men." He says, "I gain by becoming a servant to all." How wonderful, I gain by losing! And the apostle shows in the chapter that this "gain" is three-fold.

Let us note Paul's expansion of this word "gain" in the chapter. In verse 22 the Apostle eloquently writes, "I am made all things to all men that by all means I may save some." Effectual soul-winning will be the first and the great result of adjustment to the life principle our text sets before us. We shall save some, lead some to salvation by so living, says our missionary predecessor. This is a fact for God says so.

In verse 17 of our chapter the great apostle adds another incentive to this all-out unselfish devotion to Christ to which he calls us. He says, "If I do this thing willingly, I have a reward." Not only is the winning of souls wrapped up with my obedience to the principles the text sets forth — my eternal reward is involved. If I willingly devote myself to the Lord Jesus as He marks out the path in this chapter, I shall gain eternal reward.

In verse 27 of our chapter, we read, "But I keep under my body and bring it into subjection lest by any means when I have preached to others I myself shall be a castaway." In this verse another gain in consequence of self-abdication is set forth. The advantage here indicated is that of not being set aside by the Lord in the course of life as a useless vessel. A non-devoted life, a non-sacrificial life, a life without self-abdication is likely to be set aside by the Lord as being entirely useless to Him. So then if we would gain souls, if we would gain eternal rewards, and if we would avoid being set aside as valueless, unfruitful missionaries we must take the way the great apostle has indicated to us in this our text, "For though I am free from all men yet have I made myself servant unto all that I might gain the more."

A missionary once came to Cuba to assist us at a time of great need. He was a gifted man in the Spanish language and he, like no other person, could translate hymns from English to Spanish. As a teacher he was also very able. After some time he became interested in uniting permanently with the West Indies Mission. When we talked with him we made it clear that to be a member of our Mission he would have to live on the allowance all our missionaries received. He was not willing to do this, nor would he consent to live in a home comparable to those in which our missionaries lived. After the conversation with our brother we concluded we could not use him and told him so.

We could not violate the principles of self-sacrifice our God had given us as a mission to make room for a self-centered missionary. The last time I saw this man he was back here in North America without a pastorate and completely disassociated from Christian work. He was tending a machine for extricating juice from carrots as a means of livelihood. I could not help but feel that he was the Lord's castaway, at least for a time, because he was unwilling to be a servant for Jesus' sake.

Toward what conclusions does Paul's missionary pattern in I Corinthians 9 point? Does it not clearly indicate that missionary adequacy is found on a high plane of spiritual life? Surely those who feel impelled of divine love to become missionaries do not want to live on a spiritually low plane. The standard that the great missionary sets for the task of missions in this chapter seems rigorous, to be sure. Let us remember, notwithstanding, that he who commends it to his successors does so under divine inspiration, and too, that the practice it advises made Paul the greatest missionary of history.

VII

THE WOE OF MISSIONS
L. E. MAXWELL

. . . necessity is laid upon me; yea, woe is unto me if I preach not the gospel! (I Corinthians 9:16)

The Communists boast, "We do not play with words. We are realists. . . . Of our salaries and wages we keep only what is strictly necessary and give up the rest for propaganda purposes. To this propaganda we also 'consecrate' all our free time and a part of our holidays. You (Christians), however, give only a little time and hardly any money for the spreading of the Gospel of Christ. . . . Believe me, it is we who will win, for we believe in our Communist message; we are ready to sacrifice everything, even our life . . . . but you people are afraid to soil your hands."

I. OBEDIENT FAITH

What is the secret of the Communist's power? What fires him with the zeal of a crusader? He believes, poor deceived soul, that he has the cure for all economic ills. The fiery passion of the Bolsheviks to liberate their brethren and create a new world order is built upon the belief that their mission is worth dying for. Fanaticism though it be, it is fired by faith. Whittaker Chambers rightly says: "The Communist's power is the power to hold convictions and to act upon them. Communists are that

L. E. MAXWELL is the President of Prairie Bible Institute, Three Hills, Alberta, Canada. Since he has been in this school-leadership position more than 800 young people have gone forth into the mission fields of the world from P.B.I. Among these are four of his own children from a family of seven. His expressed desire is: "We are trusting that our other three will also become missionaries."

part of mankind who have recovered the power to live or die —
to bear witness — for their faith."

Theirs is a faith that illustrates "the obedience of faith." A
faith that obeys Christ is the true Christian faith. In fact there
is no other kind of faith but the faith that obeys. Any other
kind is "not another," for a faith without works is dead — no
faith at all.

"Does not your Grace think it almost useless and extravagant
to preach the Gospel to the Hindus?" asked a young clergyman
of the Duke of Wellington. The great general gave that preacher
the deserved and drastic rebuke: *What are your marching orders, sir?"*

Such trifling questions as, "Is world evangelization feasible?"
and "Do missions pay?" betray an ignorance of the first principle
of the Christian faith, namely, believing submission to the Lord
Jesus Christ as the Captain of our salvation. Fresh from His
passion our risen Lord said, "All *authority* is given unto me in
heaven and in earth. Go ye *therefore* . . . . Go ye into all the
world and preach the gospel to every creature." That command
was given by the highest authority. Observe that it is no appeal
to our manhood, no challenge to our dignity. Much less is it
good counsel, but rather it is an explicit command to be im-
plicitly obeyed. There has been far too much emphasis on *challenge* to achievement, far too little on *obedience* to command.
Failure to obey this command is to deny Christ's Lordship of the
Church and, in principle, to make void the whole Word of God.
It is this flagrant disobedience to our "marching orders" that con-
stitutes what has been termed "the crime of the century."

"Go preach" — our marching orders. "The gospel to every
creature"—a plain command. Mounting millions who have never
heard — a simple and terrifying fact. I say, "terrifying fact" —
terrifying it should be to believers — for "these millions of unsaved souls we must confront at the bar of God. What can we
do for their salvation — nay, for our own salvation from blood-
guiltiness — before the sun of life shall set?" (A. T. Pierson)

This quotation from that great missionary statesman of the

past generation brings into sharp focus the burden of our message, "The Woe of Missions." As disciples of Christ we are forever seeking to evade the imperative necessity of taking the Gospel to the lost. Our chief wickedness, of course, is lack of submission to the Lordship of Christ. We render an astounding amount of "Lord, Lord" lip-service, while we do not the things which He commands.

II. Burning Conviction

Why has the Church ceased to be militant? Where is our masculinity? Why all this effeminacy? If the Church is actually a fighting force of Christian soldiers, why are we not "as an army terrible with banners?" What has killed our desire to fight? Does it come to this, that unbelief, fatal and wicked unbelief, has killed our conviction about the absolute necessity of our message?

A distinguished church leader, as quoted by Dr. R. H. Glover, made the following impassioned appeal at the annual gathering of the officials of his denomination:

"Why is it that the interest in foreign missions is everywhere lagging and that gifts are falling off? It is because Christian people are no longer gripped by a burning conviction that men everywhere are lost without Christ. The sense of urgency, of immediate danger, of a crisis in salvation has largely disappeared. Many of our preachers no longer preach as dying men to dying men. Our forefathers believed that men everywhere without Christ were in immediate danger of facing the wrath of God. Our modern world has largely lost this urgent note in salvation. We need to restore it . . . . It is this loss of a mighty conviction about salvation and of both a present and a future disaster to the souls and to modern civilization without Christ that has cut the nerve of missionary obligation and enthusiasm." *The Bible Basis of Missions,* p. 41)

Was it John Wesley who observed that nearly all error begins with false views regarding the *state,* the *need* and the *danger* of man? The basic trouble with many today is that they are thinking outside the Book, thinking above that which is written. For us Christians the diagnosis of the Great Physician must forever remain the last word.

The pages of divine revelation declare man to be an enemy of God, a rebel against his King, "alienated from the life of God by wicked works," rejecting the reign of the Most High, and in danger of "everlasting destruction from (proceeding from) the presence of the Lord and from the glory of His power."

The vast and pressing need of this prodigal race is for peace, peace based upon reconciliation with God. But since God has declared that "the wages of sin is death" and that "He will by no means clear the guilty," it is evident that "without shedding of blood is no remission." In His atoning death, Christ has effected this reconciliation: "You, that were sometime alienated and enemies in your mind by wicked works, yet now hath he reconciled in the body of His flesh through death." And the missionary mandate from the Director-General of our campaign is to make known this reconciliation, to publish these glad tidings, to beseech men to lay down their rebellious weapons and be reconciled to the Throne through the death of heaven's beloved One.

Until these great facts fasten themselves upon us, we have no gospel. If man is not an enemy, he needs no reconciliation; if not a slave, he needs no redemption; if not a sinner, he needs no forgiveness; if not dead in sins, he needs no life; if not depraved, he needs no holiness; if not polluted and filthy, he needs no cleansing.

III. A Dynamic Gospel

If these frightful facts of man's need be so, bless God we have the one and only Gospel to meet that need. Paget Wilkes says, "It is no gospel to tell men that God merely loves good people and those that seek Him. There is not even *news* in that. The *new* thing and the *good* thing of God's message is that He loves sinners; He died for rebels; He waits to show mercy on the most openhanded sinner alive. This is news indeed and good beyond reckoning."

This Gospel is indeed good news, but good only to the man who gets it. Since there is "none other name under heaven given among men, whereby we must be saved" and since any man "without Christ" is "without hope and without God" in this world as well as in the world to come, it is imperative that Christ be preached to all men. Paul's argument for the universal necessity of the Gospel is found in Romans 10:12-15, where he asks these four unanswerable questions: *"How* then shall they call on him in whom they have not believed? and *how* shall they believe in him of whom they have not heard? and how shall they hear without a preacher? And *how* shall they preach, except they be sent?" (vss. 14 and 15a)

These questions help us to understand the apostle's feeling of necessity and "woe" when he says, *"Necessity* is laid upon me; yea, *woe* is unto me if I preach not the gospel" (I Corinthians 9:16). How urgent is this "necessity"? how serious this "woe"? Certainly Paul was overwhelmed with the urgent necessity of the Gospel. As to the "woe," Paul says in another connection, "I take you to record this day, that I am pure from the blood of all men." In comment upon this passage Lenski, the great Lutheran theologian, says, " 'Blood' is a pregnant, metonymical term for the guilt involved in bringing about death, here eternal death. On the great judgment day none of the lost from this territory shall be able to point to Paul and say that his is the guilt. Whoever may be guilty, Paul is pure from this terrible stain."

The degree of the apostle's (and the Church's) guilt involved in Paul's "woe is unto me" is a question only the All-wise can finally settle. But be sure He will settle it. That reckoning day is coming. However, there is little doubt that we have watered down that "woe" to suit our doctrinal preconceptions and to avoid being discomforted or too seriously inconvenienced. Is it not remarkable, however, that every servant of God who has been mightily used to the saving of the lost has been fully convinced not only of an eternal hell but also of his own bloodguilt-iness — "murder by neglect" — if he fails to deliver his message?

Listen to Hudson Taylor, that great pioneer of modern inter-denominational faith missions, as he meets his personal "woe." God was asking him to found a new agency to carry the Gospel to inland China. In his ears there rang continually these words: "If thou forbear to deliver them that are drawn unto death, and those that are ready to be slain (*those slipping to the slaughter* — Young); if thou sayest, Behold, we knew it not; doth not he that pondereth the heart consider it? and he that keepeth thy soul, doth not he know it? and shall not he render to every man according to his works?" (Proverbs 24:11, 12)

In the light of such Scriptures he says: "The feeling of blood-guiltiness became more and more intense. Simply because I refused to ask for them, the labourers did not come forward — did not go out to China — and every day tens of thousands were passing away into Christless graves! Perishing China so filled my heart and mind that there was no rest by day, and little sleep by night, till health broke down." He refers to this dreadful issue as a "burden so crushing — these souls, and what eternity must mean for every one of them, and what the Gospel might do, would do, for all who would believe, if we would take it to them."

The final struggle came on Sunday, June 25, 1865, when, as he relates it, "Unable to bear the sight of a congregation of a thousand or more Christian people rejoicing in their own security, while millions were perishing for lack of knowledge, I wandered out on the sands alone, in great spiritual agony; and there the Lord conquered my unbelief, and I surrendered myself for this service." Only by a complete obedience to the Captain of his salvation did Hudson Taylor find relief from this confessed and awful sense of blood-guiltiness over perishing China.

Dr. A. B. Simpson expressed his awful convictions in the following song:

> A hundred thousand souls a day
> Are passing one by one away
> In Christless guilt and gloom.
> O Church of Christ what wilt thou say
> When in that awful judgment day
> They charge thee with their doom?

IV. A God-given Sense of Responsibility

Let us come still nearer to our own generation and listen to the Rev. R. A. Jaffray as he relates his own God-given sense of responsibility to the "other sheep" of Borneo and the Celebes:

"I am returning from a trip to Borneo and the Celebes, of the Dutch Indies, in the South Seas. The Lord has taken me to 'the uttermost parts of the earth,' to some of the dark places of the world, where there is no gospel light, and where literally, 'Christ is not named,' for there is no one there who can name His name.

"I was feeling glad after two months' absence to be returning home. I felt I had done my bit, as it were; I had obeyed His command, 'Go'; I had made my report to the Board, and could now settle down again to ordinary work at Wuchow, and leave the responsibility of the perishing souls I had found in these uttermost parts to others. I had done my part, the rest was with others to take up the work or not as they felt led.

"But the Lord gave me a dream, one of those vivid dreams which leave a deep and lasting impression. I have seldom had such dreams in my life; but when He sends one, there is no question but that it is from Him.

"It was a horrible dream. I thought I was at home. I was a fugitive fleeing from justice. I thought I had stains of human blood on my hands. It seemed that the Lord Jesus was pursuing me. I was full of fear and was running for my life. The pure white snow was on the ground. I stopped and tried to wash the blood stains, the 'spots of lost souls' from my hands in the snow. I looked around, and ran again. I awoke. My first words were, 'Lord Jesus, what does this mean? I do not fear Thee, I am not running away from Thee. I have no blood stains on my hands. I am washed clean in Thy precious blood, whiter than the snow. Oh teach me what this means. What can it mean?

"At once this Scripture came to my mind, 'Son of man, I have made thee a watchman unto the house of Israel: therefore hear the word of my mouth, and give them warning from me. When I say unto the wicked, Thou shalt surely die: and thou give him not warning, nor speakest to warn the wicked man from his wicked way, to save his life: the same wicked man shall die in his iniquity: *but his blood will I require at thine hand'* (Ezekiel 3:17, 18). These are the blood spots on my hands. The blood of immortal souls is required of me till I do my part to warn them, to pay my debt and preach the Gospel to them. *'Necessity is laid upon me: yea, woe is unto me if I preach not the gospel'* (I Corinthians 9:16).

"The Lord Jesus has completely cancelled the great debt of all my sins forever, but requires me to pay my gospel debt to those who have never yet heard His message of salvation. If I warn them not, if I preach not the Gospel to them, their blood is required at my hands."

This great missionary leader of the Christian and Missionary Alliance absolved himself of bloodguiltiness by plunging back into the Dutch Indies and at length laying down his life in a Japanese internment camp in the Celebes. Who follows in his train?

The Rev. Guy Playfair, the former General Director of the Sudan Interior Mission, expresses his own personal "woe" in these four lines:

> We have a blood-bought pardon;
> 'Twas purchased at infinite cost;
> That pardon left undelivered
> Leaves men eternally lost.

VI. A SPIRIT-GIVEN COMMISSION

It must be obvious from Scripture, from missionary experience, and from the history of missions, that the Spirit of God is ever seeking to drive home upon our sluggish and selfish hearts the woe of missions. The Holy Spirit, the very spirit of obedience, is the spirit of missions. It is not surprising, then, that wherever a church experiences real revival there is forthwith a revival in missionary interest. We confess, therefore, that the only effective cure for this chronic disobedience to Christ's last command is a fresh impulse of divine life, and that such a revival impulse will come only through prevailing prayer and intercession.

Shall we then, in the meantime, only pray and wait for revival? Nay verily. Let us lay revival foundations through Bible sermons on the *Holy Spirit* and *Missions*. Let ministers and teachers press home the Spirit-filled life and the missionary message. The Bible is full of missions. Preachers and churches are Biblical in proportion as they are missionary-minded. But if our people are to think missions, they must be given the Bible basis of missions. Let us in our pulpits and Sunday schools not omit these messages. These omissions have caused the fall-off in *foreign* missions.

Christians must become convicted and convinced that *missions is the first business of the Church*. The otherwise unreached must have first place in the Church's life. Missions must have first place in her thinking, first place in her giving, and first place in her going. The Church must also put missions first in giving up and sending her own young people abroad.

VII. "Woe Is Me"

Why should it be the exception that a young person in our family or church goes to the far-flung missionary fronts? All things being equal, that should be the rule and not the exception. In time of war the fittest of our young men go to the front. To stay at home is the exception. Who will dare to say that sin's fierce war is not being waged today on all fronts and in all its fury? Woe to the slackers! Woe to all the traitors! The fight is on, O Christian soldier! Come down out of the balconies and the bleachers and get into the thick of the fight. We must all *go*, or *let* go, or *help* go. The Commander-in-chief did not say, "*Stay*," but "*Go*."

Woe unto the young man who fails to go because he thinks his talents could not be fully developed and displayed in the regions beyond.

Woe unto those older folks who regret to see a promising young man bury himself among some benighted tribe beyond the seas.

Woe unto any young man who sits waiting for a special call,

as though the Captain cried, "Sit still!" instead of "Go!" What are your marching orders, young man?

Woe unto Christians who build up bank accounts and buy comforts to no end, instead of obeying Christ's command to send His messengers into all the world.

Woe be unto Christians if they forbear to deliver those of other lands who are "slipping to the slaughter." Abraham Lincoln said, "Those who deny freedom to others deserve it not for themselves, and under a just God cannot long retain it."

> (Dare) we whose souls are lighted
> With wisdom from on high,
> (Dare) we to men benighted
> The lamp of life deny?

Woe be unto any church or denomination that builds great stately monuments of stone in this country instead of sending the Gospel to the dark parts of the earth "to win for the Lamb the reward of His suffering." Billy Graham says, "After fifty generations, only thirty-five percent of the people on the earth have heard the Gospel . . . . I know of one church which spent more than $500,000 in a building program in four years. During the same time it spent only $15,000 for foreign missions."

Woe unto such a church if this awful state of affairs is not soon corrected.

What a relief when the *"woe* of missions" becomes what I would like to call *"wed* of missions." Complete obedience, cost what it may, is better, infinitely better, than disobedience. Better a thousand times to be burdened and borne down with a great and crushing sense of responsibility for the blood of others than to seek to escape the obligations of an obedient faith.

The slavish submission of Communists to their masters in Moscow shames the average Christian with such reproach that he should cry, "Woe is me for my lukewarmness to Christ." Yet how lifeless, low and vulgar are the loyalties of the Communists in comparison with the joys of complete submission to Christ. How can tribute to a tyrant ever be compared with loving response to a Redeemer? Finally, where in all Communist captivity is there the joy unspeakable? the rivers of living water? the peace that passes understanding? Where in all earth's patriotisms is there a subjection comparable to the hilarious happiness of being Christ's captive, obedient unto death?

It is so refreshing to listen to our own graduates — over 800 of them have gone abroad — as they come back on furlough from the dark places of earth where Christ has never been named. What a joy to hear them tell of souls set free, of victories won, of trials and triumphs in the far-off lands! In spite of hardships and aging frames they have no complaints, but all alike have their hearts set on going back to the country of their adoption. Filled with Paul's woe, they are wedded to missions. We are reminded of the words of a prominent English divine who once said:

"There is nothing finer nor more pathetic to me than the way in which missionaries unlearn the love of the old home, die to their native land, and wed their hearts to the people they have served and won; so that they cannot rest at home, but must return to lay their bones where they spent their hearts for Christ. How vulgar the common patriotisms seem beside this inverted homesickness, this passion for a kingdom that has no frontage and no favoured race, the passion of a homeless Christ."

That the "*woe*" of missions may become indeed the "*wed*" of missions to the many who read these pages — is the writer's prayer.

VIII

FAR HENCE UNTO THE GENTILES
Guy W. Playfair

The Church's first and most urgent responsibility is to carry out Christ's Great Commission in taking the Gospel to the ends of the earth. The epistles contain instructions as to the conduct of the church itself — "how thou oughtest to behave thyself in the house of God" — teaching which naturally follows the formation of the church. But the Great Commission, "Go ye into all the world and preach the gospel to every creature," is not a secondary matter, nor a side issue or an added occupation of the Church. It is the Church's first and full time obligation.

Paul recognized his obligation: "I am debtor . . . I am ready to preach the gospel to you that are in Rome also." Not simply debtor to preach the Gospel fully from Jerusalem to Illyricum, a distance of fifteen hundred miles, but to preach the Gospel to the whole world.

The Church has missed the mark, has failed to carry out its first and great commission. In its apostolic days, in its first three centuries, the Church, against the most devilish opposition and fiendish persecution, prospered during the reign of ten particularly wicked Roman emperors, when hundreds of thousands of believers were slain, as well as through the brighter days of less tyrannical rulers.

The zeal and purity of the once holy Church of Christ died; then followed the Dark Ages of over twelve hundred years, but

GUY W. PLAYFAIR has been for forty years the Field Director of the Sudan Interior Mission and has directed in the great advance made on this field. From 1943-57 he was General Director and increasingly his ministry when at home has been mightily used of the Lord.

not until long after the Reformation were efforts made on the part of bold, but isolated souls to preach in the regions beyond.

We generally date modern missions from the days of Carey, from which time feeble efforts have been made to reach the heathen world. There were mighty efforts indeed on the part of individuals, and on the part of some missionary societies, but when the whole Church is considered, those efforts can only be called feeble, in the light of the fact that opportunity is afforded every generation to evangelize the world.

"Opportunity is not postponed, it is lost," eternally lost. Gone forever are the opportunities of the Church of the generations of our fathers, who might have accomplished in any one generation the great task of witnessing the Gospel to the ends of the earth. Because the opportunity to evangelize the world in each generation has been lost, millions of men have been swept into a lost eternity, without ever hearing Christ's invitation to accept His offer of eternal life. The Church must bear the blame at Christ's judgment seat. If the men of Nineveh shall rise in judgment to condemn the unbelieving generation of Christ's day, will not the lost heathen, who perish in our day, arise in judgment and condemn us for having withheld from them the precious Word of Life?

We firmly believe that if Russia could have heard the pure Gospel during the past one hundred years, the terrible system of Communism would not have arisen. But she was neglected by the Church of Christ, and the Church is reaping what she has sown.

The dark hand of Communism has already drawn the curtain across one third of the human race and the shadow of that same atheistic hand is stretched across the other two-thirds of the globe. We quote Dr. Fred Schwarz of Sydney, Australia, an authority on Communism, who says: "In 1917, Lenin, the founder of Bolshevism, was in exile in Geneva, Switzerland. He had less than forty thousand fanatical followers, scattered throughout Russia and the world. As I speak to you, the party of Lenin is in iron control of eight hundred million. It has grown from forty thousand to eight hundred million in thirty-five years. This is an increase of two million percent."

Nothing to compare with this has ever been known in the history of mankind. The Gospel was not taken to Russia. "Another has *come in his own name* and him they have received." Church of Christ, remember you will reap whatsoever you sow!

The Church, in losing its opportunity, has also been shorn of its power. "All power is given unto me in heaven and in earth . . . go ye therefore . . . lo, I am with you alway." This Scripture is quoted times without number, quite apart from its context. The *all power* is given to the Church to *witness* to the ends of the earth. It was promised to those who, in obedience, go forward, and by no manner of interpretation is the promise made to a disobedient, stay-at-home Church.

Church of Christ, repent of your iniquities, confess your sins of failure, carelessness and neglect, indifference and plain disobedience; and call upon God to forgive you as you arise in newness of life. In humility go forth to carry out your God-given commission, or take the certain dreadful consequences, not only at the Judgment Seat of Christ, but of what Dr. Schwarz calls, "The prognosis of a malignant disease." He affirms that the prognosis is so extremely serious that it renders meaningless 90% of the things we plan . . . from day to day. It is so terrifying that the most pessimistic of us is fundamentally an optimist. Every Communist is convinced that Communism has won the world. The rest is a matter of mopping up operations. Face it, Church of Christ, on your knees!

I. "FAR HENCE UNTO THE GENTILES"

In the fourth chapter of the Gospel according to John we read: "My meat is to do the will of him that sent me, and to finish his work." In our Lord's prayer of John 17:4, He said: "I have finished the work thou gavest me to do." On the Cross, as His life blood ebbed away, He cried, "It is finished."

In Acts 1:1-3 we read: "Of all that Jesus *began* both to do and teach, *until* the day in which he was taken up, *after* that he through the Holy Ghost had given commandments unto the apostles whom he had chosen. . . ." In these words of Jesus, the writers, John and Luke, have shown us that Jesus completed His own particular work, which none other could ever do, and *began* another mission which He committed to the Church, His body, for completion.

The commandments herein mentioned after His resurrection, and *"until* the day in which he was taken up," are those recorded in the gospels and Acts. (Matthew 28:16-20; Mark 16:15; Luke 24:46-48; John 20:21; Acts 1:8).

The Scriptures referred to above give His post-resurrection command to witness the Gospel to every creature.

These orders were as clear and explicit as is the fact of our purchased salvation, and are as binding on His Church today as they were on the apostles and disciples to whom they were uttered nineteen hundred years ago.

To claim, or even suggest, that it is not expedient or incumbent upon the Church today to continue to carry the Gospel to the heathen world, is utterly untenable, and the one who would evade his responsibility to carry out this command has no right to claim either John 3:16 for his salvation, or any other of the *exceeding great and precious promises.* Our salvation makes us witnesses and our witness is not complete until we reach the uttermost part of the earth.

Peter, in his sermon on the day of Pentecost (Acts 2:19), clearly showed that the promise of *all power* and *lo, I am with you alway, even unto the end of the age,* was not a local one, but unto "all that are afar off, even as many as the Lord our God shall call."

Our attention in Acts is early fixed on a young man whose name is Saul, later called Paul. Stephen is stoned, "and the witnesses laid down their clothes at a young man's feet, whose name was Saul." Of him we read in Acts 9:1, 2, "and Saul, yet breathing out threatenings and slaughter against the disciples of the Lord, went unto the high priests, and desired of him letters to Damascus to the synagogues, that if he found any of this way, whether they were men or women, he might bring them bound unto Jerusalem." Paul's own testimony is this, "And I punished them oft in every synagogue, and (R.V.) *strove to make them blaspheme* and being exceedingly mad against them, I persecuted them even unto strange cities."

Paul *in his earlier testimony,* (Acts 22:17-21), shows his own inclination to be back in Jerusalem, "And it came to pass, that, when I was come again to Jerusalem, even while I prayed in the temple, I was in a trance: and saw him saying unto me, *Make haste and get thee quickly out of Jerusalem: for they will not receive thy testimony concerning me,"* and Paul argued with the Lord (verses 19, 20), "And I said, Lord, they know that I imprisoned and beat in every synagogue them that believed on thee: and when the blood of thy martyr Stephen was shed, I also was standing by, and consenting unto his death, and kept the raiment of them that slew him." God's answer is decisive, "Depart, for I will send thee *far hence unto the Gentiles.*" That is His command to Paul in the first place, and it is here repeated, "Unto whom *now* I send thee."

"Far hence unto the Gentiles" should have been the Church's constant aim in every generation, which would have accomplished God's first purpose long ago. "Then shall the end come."

The strong language used here with Paul makes it clear that the Lord was displeased at Paul's remaining in Jerusalem. Is not this a rebuke to the Church of our day? The church's business is to witness to the ends of the earth, and not that whole congregations (perhaps 100,000 of them in America alone) should sit at home and listen to sermons Sunday after Sunday, year in and year out, decade after decade, until each church generation passes out without witnessing to the heathen world the story of God's redeeming love. If men refuse to act on the light they receive, surely that light becomes darkness.

Paul's argument with the Lord concerning his witness in Jerusalem reminds us of the arguments of even some Bible-taught Christians, against taking the Gospel to the heathen. Such arguments are worthless in God's sight, but because men do not hear God's audible voice commanding them to go, they think to evade their responsibility. It may be only when they stand ashamed and abashed, trembling and confounded, before the judgment seat of Christ, they will fully realize the frightful consequences of their disobedience to God's revealed Word. "The words that I have spoken, the same shall judge him in the last day." These words are for both saved and unsaved, and there are unfaithful Christians who will be saved, "yet so as by fire."

The Church's purpose should ever have been to follow God's plan, *"Far hence unto the Gentiles."* No other plan can ever satisfy the heart of our Lord Jesus Christ, who died for those who have never heard the good news. Is it not because the Church has shut up her heart of compassion toward the heathen world, that God is compelled to withhold the opening of the windows of blessing and staunch the rivers of living water? "Occupy till I come" is the order, while the Church for the most part, like the Prodigal Son, has wasted God's substance with riotous living, pleasure mad! Until the Church as a whole, the fundamental Church, arises in obedience to carry out God's first purpose, just so long will she continue powerless and continue to die.

If man claims Christ's promises for this age and for his own salvation, then he must accept His commands. God commandeth *all men everywhere* "TO REPENT." Does "everywhere" not include China, India, Africa, or does "everywhere" mean only England, North America, the favored western world? In the face of Christ's post-resurrection commands, such teaching is antichrist and altogether out of keeping with John 3:16, *"For God so loved the world . . ."* Was it only part of the world, we ask, and if so, *which half?*

Paul went the limit to carry the Gospel everywhere. In Romans 15:18-21 he says: "For I will not dare to speak of any of those things which Christ hath not wrought by me, to make the Gentiles obedient, by word and deed, through mighty signs and wonders, by the power of the Spirit of God; so that from

Jerusalem, and round about unto Illyricum, I have fully preached the gospel of Christ. Yea, so have I strived to preach the gospel not where Christ was named, lest I should build upon another man's foundation, but as it is written, To whom he was not spoken of, they shall see: and they that have not heard shall understand."

Until his arrest, Paul continued to preach the Gospel, *not where Christ was named,* and even then he preached in the palace at Rome, witnessing both to small and great. "I am ready," he said, "to preach the gospel to you that are in Rome also. I am not ashamed of the gospel of Christ: for it is the power of God unto salvation to every one that believeth."

He had also testified (I Timothy 1:15,16), "This is a faithful saying, and worthy of all acceptation, that Christ Jesus came into the world to save sinners; of whom I am chief. Howbeit, for this cause I obtained mercy, that in me first Jesus Christ might show forth all longsuffering, for a pattern to them which should hereafter believe on him to life everlasting."

Paul was the only one, apart from Christ, who could say, "Be ye followers of me." Paul was above everything else a missionary pattern, "Not ashamed of the gospel of Christ." He knew what had been accomplished in his own life by the Spirit of God. It was by God's Spirit he claimed to be "the chief of sinners," whom God had chosen to be the chief of saints and a pattern for all time to come. He was chosen as our pattern (I Timothy 1:16). (See I Corinthians 4:16; 11:1; Philippians 3:17; I Thessalonians 1:6; II Thessalonians 3: 7,9.) Six times he directed the Church to follow him.

II. "GO . . . AND SUFFER"

Paul's bright prospects of leadership are shown in Philippians 3:4-10 and Galatians 1:14. Nevertheless, he laid aside these prospects for a life of suffering. God told Ananias, "I will show him how great things he must suffer for my name's sake," and Paul prepared to suffer.

Too often we forget the promise, "If we suffer with him we

shall also reign with him." Can you picture the Holy Spirit informing the present-day missionary of the comforts he will enjoy! Comforts *may* come through friends, but they are not promised. The Christian worker must guard against the sin of covetousness (See Philippians 1:29).

We have seen that Paul was a *pattern*. Has the Holy Spirit changed His methods, does He not expect the missionary of today to "endure hardness as a good soldier of Jesus Christ"?

"I count all things but loss for the excellency of the knowledge of Christ Jesus my Lord: for whom I have suffered the loss of all things, and do count them but dung, that I may win Christ, and be found in him, not having mine own righteousness" (Philippians 3:8,9).

"And now, behold, I go bound in the spirit unto Jerusalem, not knowing the things that shall befall me there, save that the Holy Ghost witnesseth in every city, saying that bonds and afflictions abide me. But none of these things move me, neither count I my life dear unto myself, so that I might finish my course with joy, and the ministry, which I have received of the Lord Jesus, to testify the gospel of the grace of God . . . for I have not shunned to declare unto you all the counsel of God. . . . I have coveted no man's silver, or gold, or apparel" (Acts 20:22,23).

When his friends tried to persuade him against going up to Jerusalem the last time, Paul answered, "What mean ye to weep and to break mine heart? For I am ready not to be bound only, but also to die at Jerusalem for the name of the Lord Jesus."

Paul gives us a glimpse of his sufferings in II Corinthians 11:23-28; I Corinthians 4:9-16; II Corinthians 8:11; II Timothy 1:12-15; 3:10-12; 4:16,17. Yet in the face of all this, he exultingly writes: "I am persuaded that the sufferings of this present time are not worthy to be compared with the glory that shall be revealed in us."

Paul is now the *aged*. He has come to the end of his earthly pilgrimage. He is ready to preach in Rome and ready to die at Jerusalem! In the same confident tone he now proclaims himself as *ready to be offered up.* He is looking up at the judge's stand to receive the laurel wreath of the winner and cries, "The time of my departure is at hand, I have fought a good fight, I have finished my course, I have kept the faith." He had stated in Acts 20:24 his desire to finish his course with joy, and that course is now finished and well run. Even as he knows he must face the executioner, it is with joy he adds, "Henceforth there is laid up for me a crown of righteousness, which the Lord, the righteous judge, shall give me at that day: and not to me only, but unto all them also that love his appearing" (II Timothy 4:8).

He had earlier stated, "If we suffer, we shall also reign with him." Since suffering is a part of God's will for His people, we are compelled to believe that our comfortable home ways of living may not bring us much benefit *in that day.*

III. "Go and Sacrifice"

The promise of power given by our Lord Jesus Christ in Matthew 28:19,20 was for witnessing and was fulfilled and continued just as long as the Church remained obedient. There can be no renewed fulfillment of that promise until the Church arises in singleness of heart, in obedience to Christ's command, to carry the Gospel to the nations, and we repeat, that command is just as binding on the Church today as it was upon the apostles and disciples who heard Christ utter it.

New methods to attract young people to the Church have been tried and retried during the past forty years, but these are not God's methods. "But we will give ourselves continually to prayer and the ministry of the word" (Acts 6:4). These were the methods by which the heathen world was conquered. A return to these methods will result in a return to God's blessing upon the Church.

Elijah said to the widow, "Make me a cake first." He was God's messenger and demanded, even from the poor widow, all she had. The widow might have argued, "How cruel to compel me to give you my last morsel! Beside, I have a child to feed!"

"Without faith it is impossible to please God." Any church or individual desiring to be well pleasing to God must exercise the same faith. The result was, "the barrel of meal wasted not, neither did the cruse of oil fail," until the famine was ended.

The meaning of the story of Elijah and the widow is *"God first."* The prophet stood in God's stead and said, "Make me a cake first," and the widow obeyed. Brother Christian, God is speaking to you as you read this. Is it to be God or self first? The widow obeyed, will you?

Pastors mourn over empty pews and extra work in trying to compel fewer people to supply the funds for a dying cause. Even the salary of the pastor is threatened! The number of theological institutions which have already closed is an indication of the dying cause, i.e., "churchianity" without the radiant, powerful, faithful preaching of the New Testament evangel, which is still *the power of God unto salvation.*

Since it is impossible to please God without faith, we wonder how many churches today are pleasing Him. With the Reformation came another opportunity for the Church to testify to God's saving grace to a lost world, but for more than two hundred years little effort was made along this line. The Church was too busy at home — too busy at Jerusalem.

Slowly, all too slowly, it has dawned upon a part of the Church during the past 200 years, and more particularly during the past 50 years, that it is its duty to obey Christ's last command. The achievements of missions during the latter period, especially during the last 30 years, have been splendid. The work of Bible Societies, through missionary translators, has been no less glorious, and these together have translated the Bible or part thereof into more than 1150 languages. Nor does this tell the whole story. Hundreds of tribes have learned one or more of the main languages in certain countries, and it is safe to say that from fourteen to fifteen hundred tribes are hearing the Gospel, if not in their own mother tongue, at least in a tongue which they have learned, and into which the Scriptures have been translated. Charles Wesley wrote:

> O for a thousand tongues to sing
> My great Redeemer's praise.

His great Redeemer's praises *are* being sung today by vastly more than a thousand tongues!

We rejoice at the progress of the Gospel and at these magnificent achievements, but we deplore the fact that only a comparatively small proportion of even the fundamental Churches are alive to missions! This is plain disobedience.

With an open Bible in which Christ's commands stand out clearly; with missionaries returning to the homeland to tell the story; with missionary literature, and yet no general response, is it not mockery? Is it possible that God is well pleased with His Church, which from generation to generation neglects His Word, treats His commands lightly, shuts up her heart of compassion to the heathen, and refuses to warn the wicked of impending doom? We believe not.

Of those faithful ones our Lord says, "Thou hast a few names even in Sardis which have not defiled their garments; and they shall walk with me in white: for they are worthy" (Revelation 3:4).

The Church has always had a witness and as Israel had its seven thousand, even in the days of the worst apostasy, so the Lord now has His faithful ones. Through them the Gospel is being slowly taken to the heathen world by those who go and those who faithfully support them by their prayers and by their gifts. Through lack of men and money, missions have taken one hundred years to reach from the coast to Central Africa — thus in one hundred years having only accomplished what should have been done in ten to twenty years. Compare this with the progress of Communism, forty thousand to eight hundred million in thirty-five years!

We quote from an article in the *Evangelical Christian* of November, 1953:

COMMUNISM IN LATIN AMERICA

We communists do not play with words. We are realists and, seeing that we are determined to achieve our object, we know how to obtain the means. Of our salaries and wages, we

keep only what is strictly necessary, and we give up the rest
for propaganda purposes. To this propaganda we also "consecrate" all of our free time, and a part of our holidays.

You, however, give only a little time and hardly any money
for the spreading of the Gospel of Christ. How can anyone
believe in the supreme value of this Gospel if you do not
practice it, if you do not spread it, and if you sacrifice neither
time nor money for it?

Believe me, it is we who will win, for we believe in our
Communistic message and we are ready to sacrifice everything,
even our life, in order that social justice shall triumph. But
you people are afraid to soil your hands.

Were our Christianity as vital as that of the apostolic days
the open world could be fully and easily reached in this generation. Of them we read, "With great power gave the apostles
witness of the resurrection of the Lord Jesus: and great grace
was upon them all."

Today, Christians number millions in every great Protestant
country, yet few of Christ's people will go to the heathen or
Moslem world with the Gospel and few are prepared to sacrifice
in order that they might send them. It is not for Jesus' sake
first, but for self!

IV. Go and Serve

Not a generation passes in which the world could not be
evangelized. Any generation could evangelize the world in the
generally accepted twenty-five years of its own generation, and
therefore, as each generation neglects taking the Gospel to the
heathen world, it brings upon itself its own condemnation.
"Every one of us shall give an account of himself to God," and
"God is not mocked, for whatsoever a man soweth that shall he
also reap," is true of the Church, and God cannot look with
complacency upon continued disobedience. We repeat, Israel
sowed the wind and reaped the whirlwind each time she departed from God, and while He bare long with her, He
punished her, finally casting her out of His sight.

"Judgment must begin at the house of God" is not an Old
Testament warning, but is quoted from I Peter 4:17. God's
judgment upon Israel was no light matter. Ananias and his

wife, as individuals, were judged in a moment, and their judgment was swift and terrible.

To Israel God had said in Leviticus 25:23, "The land is mine," and in Leviticus 25:4, "But the seventh year shall be a Sabbath of rest unto the land, a Sabbath for the Lord; thou shalt neither sow thy field nor prune thy vineyard."

Yet Israel obeyed not this command, and after they were utterly banished, never to return, Judah followed much the same course. She regarded not this law, *much as the Church today regards not the command of Christ to take the Gospel to the heathen,* seeming to think it a matter of little moment, not realizing that it is God's first and supreme business.

There are many who profess to be looking for the return of Christ at any moment, yet are not concerned, nor give particular heed to witness or send witnesses to the unreached heathen. We are persuaded that for such, the coming of Christ will not be an unmixed joy, but rather a solemn event. Such should realize *now,* before it is too late, that when our Lord Jesus said, "The words which I have spoken the same shall judge him in the last day," these words include His post-resurrection command to give the Gospel to the uttermost part of the earth.

How great is the disaster if you or I refuse to obey! No human mind can conceive the dimensions of our folly to pass lightly over God's revealed will for the salvation of the heathen. This is its unspeakable importance because the eternal destiny of God's own loved creation is at stake. No words spoken by human tongue can tell or portray the importance of our heeding Christ's command. There is only one thing to do and that is, go and tell them! God wants to use you and me to save His lost creatures.

Christian, when God says, "Bring ye all the tithes into the storehouse, that there may be meat in mine house" He means it. Bring the tithes of money; of time; of love; of prayer; of service; of thanksgiving; of praise; of intercession, "Bring *all* the tithes into the storehouse."

Some years ago three men, one of them a doctor, were

entombed in a mine in Eastern Canada. The news was flashed across the world, as hundreds of men went to work to extricate them. They worked with all the energy humanly possible and with all the desire of men seeking to save their companions. There was a sympathetic United States, Canada, England and the world. News was broadcast continually regarding the progress made by the would-be rescuers. Finally, after days and nights of labor, contact was made with the entombed men, when it was learned that one of them had died. The fact that two were still alive encouraged the hundreds of workers to continue with increased energy. At last the two men were brought forth safely.

Was it worth while? Had it been you or I, or some of our loved ones, we would have thought it was worthwhile to spend all that time, sympathy, energy, and money! And it was worth while many times over, just to extend the lives of those men a few years longer in this sin-cursed world! Then, my Christian reader, is it not ten thousand times ten thousand more worth while to send the Gospel to the heathen world, to deliver men from the thraldom and *power of Satan unto God* that they, too, may *receive forgiveness of sins;* that they be delivered not only to live a few years longer in this life, but throughout all eternity, to glorify the Lord, who for them has shed His precious blood, and who says, "Deliver him from going down to the pit. I have found a ransom"? Beside, there is the solemn fact that our Lord Jesus *commanded* us to go and tell them!

> Go and tell them; go and tell them;
> Jesus died for sinful men.
> Go and tell them; go and tell them;
> That He's coming back again.

"We've a story to tell to the nations," is often sung at missionary meetings. We would like to add one verse to those already written, and it would be:

> We've a pardon to give to the nations
> Which was purchased at infinite cost,
> A pardon as yet undelivered,
> Which leaves them eternally lost.

Jesus purchased our pardon. "This is my blood of the new testament, which is shed for many for the remission of sins." He committed this pardon to His Church as its only custodian, to deliver to a lost world, and said, "Go . . . and preach the gospel to every creature."

Suppose the Governor of a State should write out a pardon for a condemned man, and this pardon were withheld by the custodian until the prisoner had been executed. Of what use would be the pardon? What would we think of the man who failed to deliver such a pardon? Would he not be held in utter contempt, even by the world? The Church is in the same position today as that custodian, and has not delivered the pardon to the heathen world!

Of what use has Christ's pardon been to the billions of people who have died without receiving it? Jesus Christ died in vain for them because the Church has shelved the pardon, and in thousands of individual churches, that pardon is forgotten as far as the heathen world is concerned. It is, therefore, *an undelivered pardon.*

Most fundamental Christians are looking for the return of Christ. Suppose our gracious Lord were to return today and ask, as He certainly must ask His followers, why His command to preach His redemption story to every tongue and people was not carried out; why each saved one did not do all in his power to *Go* or to *Give* and to *Pray* that others go and tell them?

My fellow Christian, are you prepared to give Him an answer — a satisfactory answer of obedience to that command? If not, then, for Jesus' sake, for God's glory, for the salvation of the heathen, and for the defeat of Satan by robbing him of his spoils, and for the hastening of Christ's return, do take action *NOW.* Do not sleep until you have settled it with God and made up your mind.

IX

WHY ARE THE HEATHEN LOST?
T. Titcombe

How often we are asked, "Do you believe that if the heathen have never heard the Gospel of the Lord Jesus Christ, that they will be lost?" I would like to answer this question from that wonderful portion of God's Word — Romans 10. In the first three verses, Paul says of the children of Israel: "Brethren, my heart's desire and prayer to God for Israel is, that they might be saved. For I bear them record that they have a zeal of God, but not according to knowledge. For they being ignorant of God's righteousness, and going about to establish their own righteousness, have not submitted themselves unto the righteousness of God."

What Paul said to the Jews is also true of the heathen of Africa, indeed for those people anywhere in the world that we call primitive or heathen. It has been my privilege to travel in Africa, and to have lived among the lowest type of people in that dark land: among the cannibals, the headhunters, and the Mohammedans. I have never found in any tribe, no matter how low they may have fallen, or what their background may have been, but that they had a name for God. It is true that they sacrifice to their "gods," but being ignorant of God's righteousness they have made a way of their own. Why? Because of ignorance, for they had no knowledge of the true way of salvation as it has been provided by the Lord Jesus Christ. They worship ignorantly with human sacrifices, sacrifices of

"Tommy" Titcombe went to Africa under the Sudan Interior Mission in 1907 and pioneered in this field. He is now Deputation Secretary in the homeland and his ministry has laid the burden of missions upon many. Few men have stirred the churches of America for missions as has this man.

animals, sacrifices of birds, sacrifices of grain and beer and almost anything that might be brought as an offering, all being made in their worship to the "unknown God."

The apostle Paul spoke about that when he preached his sermon on Mars Hill. He told how they have a zeal, both pagan and Mohammedan, but they have no peace, no hope, no knowledge of God's way of salvation.

Returning to the tenth chapter of Romans, we see where Paul builds up a most wonderful argument, precept upon precept, until in the thirteenth verse he has this climax: "For whosoever shall call upon the name of the Lord shall be saved." I can almost see the glow upon his face as he stands before these people and declares this wonderful truth that "whosoever shall call upon the name of the Lord shall be saved." This truth of "whosoever" (that wonderful word) is found also in the third chapter of John's gospel, and the sixteenth verse: "For God so loved the world." Surely that takes in the Africans, it takes in the lowest pagan and the Continent of Africa and sweeps across the world. God so loved the world that He gave His only begotten Son that "whosoever shall call upon the name of the Lord shall be saved."

But my dear friends, almost the moment Paul comes out with this declaration, that "whosoever shall call upon the name of the Lord shall be saved," a quiver creeps into his voice and he comes back with these words: "How then shall they call on him of whom they have not heard? how shall they hear without a preacher? and how shall they preach except they be sent?"

May I bring to you out of these last verses just three pictures?

I. Waiting for the Message

The first picture that I would like to bring to you is that of the pagans of Africa waiting for the message. If you want to see a picture of the heathen world, turn to the fifth chapter of the gospel of John and read in verses 3 and 4: "Now there is at Jerusalem by the sheepmarket a pool, which is called in the Hebrew tongue Bethesda, having five porches. In these lay a great multitude of impotent folk, of blind, halt, withered, waiting for moving of the water." This is a picture of the Africans, waiting for the moving of the water, or waiting for the Gospel of the Lord Jesus Christ to come with all its healing, purifying power.

The condition of these people as they wait for the moving of the water is pathetic. They are blind, they are halt, they are withered. The African is blind with superstition, he is halt with cruelty, and he is withered with witchcraft.

How can I bring to your attention the condition of Africa as I know it, the condition of Africa as I have seen it? Let me try to illustrate it. One morning at three o'clock, someone outside my door cried out "Ooh ye bo, ooh ye bo" — "white man, white man." I jumped out of bed and saw two boys outside lying on the ground. When I went outside one of them said, "White man, come quickly." Putting on a few clothes, thinking that I was going down to the village, I went back outside the door and the boys started to run.

"Where are we going?" I called after them.

"To Koro," they replied. That was six miles away and I knew that I would not be able to run six miles, but I followed them as quickly as I could, running and walking, but still the two boys were well ahead of me.

They met me just outside the village, and said, "Oh white man, you are too late." "Too late for what?" I asked.

"Wa wo," — "come and look." We went toward the center of the village and there I saw a woman stripped of all clothing, moving forwards and backwards and wailing as only a mother of Africa knows how. Constantly she was crying out, "Where are my babies, my babies?" I approached her and put my hand on her head, I said, "What is the matter?"

"I want my babies," she replied.

"Tell me where your babies are and I will get them."

I might as well have told her that I would get the sun or the moon for her, for I could have gotten them just as quickly. It was then that they told me the story.

During the night the woman had given birth to twin babies, and with her newly awakened maternal love she tried to hide them under her own body. Yes, there is almost as much maternal love in Africa as there is at home. This woman loved her babies, wanted to keep her babies, but she was born in Africa, and after giving birth to the twins she knew that she must hide them or lose them.

When she began to cry for these white men who she thought might be able to help her save her children, two boys said that they would go and bring me. When the boys arrived at the hut so far ahead of me they heard the woman still calling, "White man, white man." The people of the village had burst into the hut, had kicked the woman to one side like so much refuse, and taking those children out into the open bush, they cut their heads off and stuffed them under a pot.

Friends, why did they do this? The woman wanted to keep her babies. The woman loved her babies. Then why sacrifice them? Because of superstition, the superstition that has blinded the minds and the hearts of the people of Africa for centuries.

Not only are they blinded by superstition, but they are "halt" with cruelty.

I was studying in my home one evening when someone came to the doorway and said, "White man, will you come to town?" I was no sooner outside the door of my hut when I heard the screaming and shouting in the town nearby. When I got there I fell back in horror. I saw big burly men who had taken the straw off of the roofs of some of the huts. As I arrived they were setting fire to great bundles of the dried grass and using them as lighted torches, they applied them to the body of a woman who was lying on the ground.

I am not very big, but what I lack in stature I can make up in volume! I gave a shout and those men scattered to their huts like rabbits to their holes. Then I knelt beside the woman and speaking quietly into her ear, I asked, "Why are they putting this fire to your body?"

She lifted up a mangled hand. Whispering she said, "I am a leper."

"Well," I said, "we have all kinds of lepers in the town of Egbe. Why should they be putting fire to you and not to the rest of them?"

Then she replied, "White man, I am a stranger." It was enough. They could be cruel to a strange leper.

I had no place for her to stay but near my hut there was a small cattle hut that was used only at night time. I cleaned it up, sent a boy to get the mat off my floor and got the woman settled there and took her some food. Yes, and as I fed her that physical food, I fed her also from the Book of books, talking to her about the Lord Jesus Christ. That night the cattle were not able to use the hut but my old leper friend, covered with an old blanket, slept there safely and quietly.

In the dawn of the early morning, I went out to see how my patient was but when I peeked into the hut, I found she was gone. I looked everywhere for her but could not find her. Then someone said, "White man, you will find her outside the village wall," and going outside, I saw the woman — burned to death! Why? She was a leper. She was born in a land where the people are still waiting for the message of love.

Oh friends, how often we hear the people at home saying, "Leave the heathen alone. They are perfectly happy. They are perfectly satisfied." But they are "the blind, the halt, the withered."

They are withered with the worship of demonism and witchcraft.

Going to the town one day, I heard someone cry "Abi pami." The heartbreaking cry stopped me and I dashed over to the hut and knocked down the door and looking inside, I beat a hasty retreat. The stench was terrible and the sight was awful. Getting a second breath, I went back in and approached a man who sat with his hands through a block of wood. He was nailed to that wood. Farther off in the hut, I saw an old woman and I said to her, "What is the meaning of this?"

She said, "My son."

"Your son? Then why is he nailed to this block of wood?"

"He has a demon," she replied, "and the witch doctor has compelled me to nail him to this block of wood." The young man, Jegadi, looked up into my face and he cried out "Abi pami, white man, I am hungry."

I went over to try to loose the young man from his block of wood, but the mother fell at my feet and said, "White man, if you loose him or let him go, the witch doctor will murder every member of my family." Nevertheless, I let him loose and for some time after that Mrs. Titcombe cared for him and saw him restored to health and strength again.

Friends, this is the condition of Africa. Are the heathen lost? They are not only lost, but they are suffering as a result of being under the control of the power of the enemy of souls.

II. WAITING FOR THE MESSENGER

Let us go back to the fifth chapter of John and read this: "For an angel went down at a certain season into the pool, and troubled the waters; whosoever then first after the troubling of the water stepped in, was made whole of whatsoever disease he had." Yes, provision had been made for those multitudes who were lying along the side of the pool. God had made provision without money and without price and yet here was a man who had been lying there for no less than thirty-eight years. God has made provision for those who are blind with superstition in Africa. God has made provision for those who are halt with cruelty from paganism. God has made provision for those under the power of demonism and witchcraft. Yes, "God so loved the world," he loved the African, "that He gave His only begotten Son." "How shall they call upon Him without a preacher?" We have the message. God has provided that without money and without price. God has provided the message by sending His only begotten Son into the world for you and for all mankind. But how can these others hear without a preacher. God has only one method of taking the Gospel to these people and that is through your lips and mine. It is by your feet and mine. Before that message can go to Africa, the Lord Jesus Christ needs a messenger, since although the remedy has been provided, it is without effect upon the African until the messenger takes it. In the story that we are reading in John 5:7; there are these words, "For when the water is troubled, there is no man to put me into the pool." Now friends, the question comes to your heart and mine — Will the simple Gospel of the grace of God reach the people of Africa? Not unless we are willing to go. Let me take you for a moment to the little village of Koro.

Mrs. Titcombe and I were married in Africa after I had been out there for eight years. The Lord gave us a set of twins. When our twins were three years of age, Mrs. Titcombe and I left to work at Koro. We went into the area where they had the practice of cutting off the heads of twin babies and putting them in pots. Our twins, alive and frisky and happy, were allowed to play with the pagan children. While we were in that area of scrub or brush, I turned over some seventy-five pots, each one with the remains of twins that had been murdered because of that dreadful superstition that demons were responsible for multiple births. When we came out of that area and Mrs. Titcombe and I got to our hut, she fell on her knees and began to weep as if her heart would break.

"What is the matter, honey?" I asked.

"Tommy," she replied, "if I had been born in Africa instead of America, my little babies would have been out there in one of those dreadful pots!" Just then an old man whose hands had been stained with human blood came to our hut. Mrs. Titcombe couldn't face him at the moment but I went out and began talking to him. Our twin girl came up and I said to her, "Greet the old man." Then she said, "Oh kuo baba" (Hello father). He looked around at her, then said, "Why, she understands our language!"

Just then her twin brother came out. When he saw the twin boy he put his thumb over his lips and said, "Why, they are twins."

I said, "Of course they are twins."

"They are human."

I said, "Of course they are human."

Then he replied, "Well, we believe that when a woman gives birth to twins, she is no longer a human being but an animal. Therefore we murder the babies and drive the mother out to the bush." It was just as heartless as that.

Mrs. Titcombe and I went home. When I came back again to that same area, I was sitting under a tree one day when along came a young man. We sat and talked and he told me his name, and I began to tell him about the Lord Jesus Christ. He turned to me after a while and said, "White man, does God know what is on my fingers?"

I said to him, "Ajawi, God not only knows what is on your fingers, but God knows what is in your heart. But," I said, "Christ died for you, and shed His blood, and the blood of Jesus Christ will make your heart as white as the clouds of the sky." A short time later I was privileged to lead that man to Christ.

Will this message do anything? It changed the heart of the murderer into a follower of the Lord Jesus Christ. And for it, Ajawi suffered. He had his crops burned. He had his house burned, because he had left the old paganism for the new way. But if we go to the little village of Koro today, what do we find? Instead of a place where where they murdered twins, they have two churches, where there are hundreds who are rejoicing in the knowledge that their sins have been forgiven and that they have a glorious hope of someday seeing the Lord Jesus as He is, and they will be like Him!

Another time, I had an experience with a man afflicted with leprosy. Leprosy is a dreadful disease. It is a true type of sin. But this man came to my home under the influence of liquor and fell into the hut and fell asleep. I let him sleep, but after he woke up he looked at me and said, "Where am I?"

I said, "You are in my home."

He was ashamed, but I had the privilege of bringing the

message to him and began to talk to him about the Lord Jesus Christ and soon I was able to lead him to the Saviour. He came to the church for a little while but soon his ears had gone, his nose had gone. The people came and asked me if I would make him sit under a tree rather than in the church. It was the hardest thing that I had ever had to do, but when I talked to him he said, "It's all right, white man." So he sat under the tree and listened as I spoke and preached in the church.

Then one day I received a letter from the representative of the British and Foreign Bible Society, in which he said, "Mr. Titcombe, may I come and speak to your people and present to them the work of the British and Foreign Bible Society?" These were cannibal people, these were pagans, these were the lowest type of human beings, yet now that they had been redeemed by the blood of the crucified One, the representative of the B. and F.B.S., the Rev. A. W. Banfield said, "Let me come and present the work." My immediate reply was, "Come." The next morning he stood before the people and spoke for two hours with me interpreting for him into the native language. And there was Eli, the leper, sitting under his tree. One of my elders jumped to his feet and said, "White man, will you give us something definite to do?"

"Yes," he said, "but it is too much for you to do."

"What is it?"

"Reach the Jaba tribe. We are trying to print the Scriptures for the Jaba tribe and it will cost so much money." The elder looked down for a moment, then he said, "We cannot pay all that." But another elder said, "White man, will you give us time?"

"Yes, we will give you at least two months."

After I dismissed the congregation, I went back home and I had been there just a few minutes when a husky voice cried out, "White man." Going outside, I found Eli, the leper. He said, "White man, will you send to my farm? Will you ask the woman there to sell half of my farm?" I replied "What for?"

"I want to send a book up into the Jaba tribe. I want to help pay for a book to go to the Jaba tribe."

"No," I said, "Eli, I will not do that for you."

Two months later when I was about to go into the church this same husky voice though now very weak said, "Kokba, white man, will you take this?" He dropped into my hand an amount of money in the West African currency which came to about seventy-five cents. I said, "What is this?"

He said, "I sent the woman to the farm and they sold it. I sold everything I had and I want to give this to Jesus for what He has done for me." It was only a few days later that I was called to his hut and there he lay dying. I took his head upon my lap and looked into that mutilated face. He looked up at me and said, "White man, thank you for telling me of the One who died for me." Yes friends, that is the work of the messenger.

Yes, thank God, the Gospel of the grace of God can break the power of demonism and give glorious freedom. I have seen men demon-possessed. I could take you to see a demon-possessed woman chained to a block of wood for no less than eight years. Why? Simply because she was demon-possessed. They said if we let her go she would tear the place to pieces. They fed her like a dog but we know that the message of the Cross can break the power of demonism and set all gloriously free. Yes, that is why we go to Africa.

I have been telling you about a leper. In Nigeria alone there are 500,000 lepers unreached, untouched. I had a most pitiful letter from one of my fellow missionaries (who works in Ethiopia) only last week. He said, "Tommy, will you do something that we might be able to build a mission station among the desert people where there are thousands of lepers? Because of this dread disease, we can take them into our leprosarium and there reach them with the Gospel of the Lord Jesus Christ." Oh, will you help us that we might be able to build a station?

Friends, I am getting old. I know that I can never go back to that land again. No, but while I have breath in this old body of mine, I am going to do what I can to urge you to help us reach the people.

But, you may say, Tommy, you have told us of the people waiting. You have told us about someone to take the message. But what can we do? This question is often asked me in meetings. If I were only younger, I would gladly go back to Africa. If I had my youth again, I would gladly be there to reach them with the Gospel. But I cannot go. But some others can go. Listen, the Scripture says, "Ye shall be witnesses unto me, both in Judea and Jerusalem, in all Samaria, and unto the uttermost part of the earth." Even if you cannot go, that does not excuse you. When the Word says, "Go ye into all the world," it means that. But you may say with me, "I'm too old. I've got a family." Well, you can help send someone! That could be your part. And here is the third picture.

III. Waiting to Be Sent

Christian friends, just remember that there are scores of young people, waiting, waiting to be sent. They have the message and they want to go, but there is no one to send them. How can they go unless they be sent, and how can they be sent unless you stand behind them by prayer and by gift? "Pray ye therefore the Lord of the harvest that he send forth labourers into his harvest." Yes, that is your work, to pray and to send. Let me close with these words. I am now over seventy years of age. I know it won't be too long before I see the Lord and I'm going to look upon Him who loved me and gave Himself for me. But some time ago, someone was willing to send me.

I well remember going into a village called Ife where I went about once every year to baptize the converts. The responsibility of so many villages and churches made it impossible for us to visit more than about once a year. On one of these visits, one young man came to me and I questioned him thus, "How long have you been converted?" He said, "About two years." I asked him many questions which I would not dare ask the average Christian at home and then I said, "Do you believe in the coming of the Lord Jesus?"

He said, "I surely do."

"Would you love to see your Jesus?" I questioned him.

He said, "Be ko (no)."

When I asked him why he replied, "I just don't want to be baptized." Then he started to walk back to the village. I detained him. "Wait a minute. You have been under instruction for two years and now I ask you if you'd like to see Jesus today and you answered no. Why? Have you been drinking beer? Have you committed adultery?" To each of my questions he replied, "No, white man."

"Then why do you not want to see Jesus?"

Then he gave a reply that staggered me, "I have been converted now for two years and if Jesus were to come today, I would have nothing to lay at His feet!"

Friends, if Jesus were to come today, what do you have to lay at His feet? A year later I went back into that same town. The first one before me was this young man whom I hadn't baptized the year before. The first question I asked was, "Son, would you like to see Jesus today?" He immediately replied "Wa whoo (yes, emphatically)." There came three young men with him and he said, "White man, if Jesus were to come today I would have these souls to lay at His feet!"

May I ask this question in closing? Jesus may come today. What have you to lay at His feet? You say you cannot go, but you can pray and you can give to help send others to take your place.

How well I remember a service in a small town in Canada. Following the service, we had gone to the home of an elder who was very ill. We were standing around his bed and talking together.

Then one of the elders spoke, "What are we going to do for this missionary work?

I said, "Why don't you support a missionary?"

One of them replied, "How can we support a missionary?"

My reply was, "There's enough money around this bed to support more than one missionary." One of those men, a farmer, turned and said, "Listen, I am a tobacco farmer and after these services I am going to pull my tobacco barn down and I am going into real farming." I saw him a short time ago. He is not only supporting one missionary. He is supporting two. He said, "Tommy, I don't grow tobacco, I just grow tomato plants. I not only have more money now than I ever did but now I am supporting two missionaries and someday I believe I am going to have something to lay at His feet."

How about you, friends? Let Jesus have your life, your prayers, and your funds that His name might be preached to the uttermost part of the earth. God bless you.

X

HOW TO FIND GOD'S WILL ABOUT MISSIONS
G. Allen Fleece

"In this book alone, my son, you can find the answer to all of life's problems," were the words that a boy once read on the flyleaf of the Bible that had just been handed to him as a present from his parents. Years enough have passed since then for the boy to prove in his own experience that those words can be taken at face value. To him that fact is priceless. Let it be so to you as we think for a little while about the problem of finding out if God wants me to be a missionary. The Bible has the answer.

"Then said Jesus unto them again, Peace be unto you: as my Father hath sent me, even so send I you. And when he had said this, he breathed on them, and saith unto them, Receive ye the Holy Ghost: Whose soever sins ye remit, they are remitted unto them; and whose soever sins ye retain, they are retained" (John 20:21-23).

This is serious business. Do you have peace with God? Then you are in a serious position, for it is to those who know peace that the Lord Jesus Christ speaks these words. Have your own sins been remitted? Then you are responsible for remitting the sins of others. It can only be termed a tragedy when a Christian, having found the peace of God in sins forgiven, does not have ears to hear what Christ says next.

Do not let your life be wasted because you stopped with

G. Allen Fleece is the President of the Columbia Bible College, Columbia, S. C. There is a constant procession of young people going forth from this school unto the various mission fields. The school has a strong missionary program.

"Peace be unto you," but make it count for all eternity because you heed what Jesus says next: "even so send I you."

Read again these three verses. Do you see clearly what follows our peace in each verse?

There is *our commission* (v. 21); *our enduement of power* to carry out the commission (v. 22); and *our responsibility for a lost world* (v. 23).

The Great Commission

This commission is John's account of what is generally called "The Great Commission." The Great Commission is given five times in the New Testament; once in each of the four gospels and also in Acts 1:8. Though there are differences in some details and in the circumstances when Christ gave each, the thought is essentially the same. All five accounts command the evangelization of the whole world.

Here in John this commission is very personal: "As my Father hath sent me, even so send I you." We are reminded that the Father sent the Son that men might not perish but have everlasting life (John 3:16). It is "even so" that Christ sends us. Our Lord makes us His partners in this glorious task of keeping men from perishing.

Our Part

Of course our part in this task is quite different from His. His part was to die on the Cross as the Lamb of God to make atonement with His precious blood for the sins of the world, while our part is to proclaim this fact to all men, beseeching them to be reconciled to God. Yet, though each part is different, both are necessary. For it will not profit people for Jesus to die for them unless they believe in Him, "and how shall they believe in Him of whom they have not heard? and how shall they hear without a preacher? and how shall they preach, except they be sent?" (Romans 10:14, 15). It is necessary that we do our part in making it possible for people to hear so they will "not perish but have everlasting life." The Lord Jesus has done His part, and now we must do ours.

The Holy Spirit Is Our Power

We could never carry out such a commission in our own might or power. Accordingly, in verse 23 we read that we have been given the Holy Spirit to enable us to obey our Lord's command. This is the same message that we find in Acts 1:8: "But ye shall receive power, after that the Holy Ghost is come upon you; and ye shall be witnesses unto me, both in Jerusalem, and in all Judea, and in Samaria, and unto the uttermost part of the earth." In the person and presence of the Holy Spirit we have "power . . . . unto the uttermost."

Our Solemn Responsibility

Verse 23 places upon us a solemn responsibility for the eternal destinies of men. Their sins will not be remitted unless we remit them (by taking the Gospel to them). If we withhold the Gospel from them, we withhold salvation from them. It is for this cause that God said to Ezekiel: "When I say unto the wicked, Thou shalt surely die; and thou givest him not warning, nor speakest to warn the wicked from his wicked way, to save his life; the same wicked man shall die in his iniquity; but his blood will I require at thine hand. Yet if thou warn the wicked, and he turn not from his wickedness, nor from his wicked way, he shall die in his iniquity; but thou hast delivered thy soul" (Ezekiel 3:18, 19).

Two Questions

In the light of these three verses from John's gospel we should arrive at the answer to two questions, and these answers should solve our problem of knowing what is God's will for us with regard to the mission field. The first question concerns a decision that we do not have to make; the second, a decision that we do have to make.

The Decision We Do Not Make

Shall I spend my life for the purpose of world evangelization?

This is a decision we do not make because it has already

been made. Whether we spend our lives for the purpose of reaching all men with the Gospel is not optional. Christ has commanded every Christian to do just this.

Now there are many different ways of accomplishing this one purpose, and we shall refer more particularly to them later. But, regardless of the particular job for the Lord, must be the evangelization of the whole world.

There is a sense in which the motto, "Every Christian a missionary," is very true. The Church does not have many things to do, but one thing, the carrying out of the Great Commission.

That every Christian must live his life for the purpose of spreading the Gospel is shown to be true, not only from this command of our Lord, but also from the fact that all men are lost without Jesus Christ. This awful need is such that no Christian could spend his life in the will of God without having a vital part in meeting it.

Perhaps this is just the reason why many have not clearly admitted that every person on earth, capable of moral judgment, who dies without receiving the Lord Jesus Christ, goes to hell. To face this fact and accept it would put people into a corner where there would be no choice of living for any purpose than to reach with the Gospel the perishing millions of earth.

Why the Heathen Are Lost

And yet this is just what the Bible says to be true about the lost condition of all people everywhere. Even those who have not had a chance to hear the Gospel and accept Jesus are lost and without any other hope. For though they have not rejected the Gospel, they have rejected the light of creation (Romans 1:20), and the light of conscience (Romans 2:14, 15), so that they are without excuse.

If there is a way for the heathen to be saved without hearing the Gospel and accepting Christ, then Jesus is a luxury that men may receive, not a necessity that they must receive. "Neither is there salvation in any other: for there is none other name under heaven given among men, whereby we must be saved" (Acts 4:12).

Have you ever faced the reality of what this means? It is estimated that approximately 40,000,000 people die each year in heathen lands without hearing the Gospel — more than 3,000,000 each month, or 100,000 each day. This very day which we have spent in the manifold blessings of salvation, 100,000 people have slipped out into a Christless eternity. There will never be another chance to go to them, or pray for them, or send some one to them. It was this vision that caused Dr. A. B. Simpson to write:

> They're passing, passing fast away,
> A hundred thousand souls a day,
> In Christless guilt and gloom.
> O Church of Christ, what wilt thou say
> When, in the awful judgment day,
> They charge thee with their doom?

No, we do not have to decide the question, "Shall I spend my life for the purpose of world evangelization?" In the light of Christ's command, to do so is binding upon every Christian; and in the light of the millions who are perishing without the only Saviour, we realize that a just God could leave us no choice in the matter.

However there is another question of far-reaching importance that we are to answer. Let us face next

The Decision We Do Make

"Where and how shall I spend my life for world evangelization?"

God has a perfect plan for each of our lives, and according to that plan there is one kind of service in which God can best use each of us in reaching those who have never heard the Gospel. For some, this service would be to go in person to the mission field; for others, it would be some work at home — in a church, or in business, or as a Christian wife and mother, or in some other service for Him. The important thing is to find God's place wherever and whatever it be.

If you are in that place, even though it should prove to be at home, God can use you there to reach the ends of the earth to a greater degree than in any other place. If you do not take that place, then your life, no matter how prominent, will be a tragic failure.

How to Find God's Place

How, then, can we find this place? Suppose we look at the way a young man named Isaiah found it for himself: "Also I heard the voice of the Lord, saying, Whom shall I send, and who will go for us? Then said I, Here am I; send me." We usually stop here when we quote this passage, but if we do we miss the whole point. Read the first part of the next verse — "And he said, Go, and tell this people" (Isahiah 6:8, 9).

If God should say to you as you are surveying the whole world with all its peoples and tongues, and wondering to which people at home or abroad He wants you to go, "I want you to go to this people," would not that settle the whole matter? That is exactly what God did say to Isaiah when He said, "Go, and tell this people," and He is eager to do just the same for us, for He is no respecter of persons.

We will certainly reach this place of God's clear call if we follow the same path that Isaiah followed. Did you notice the step he took? First, there was Isaiah's willingness to go anywhere for the Lord, and do anything. This is expressed in his answer, "Here am I, send me."

When Isaiah said those words God had not yet told Isaiah where He wanted him to go. Indeed He had not even spoken to Isaiah, but had simply been sending out a universal cry to know who would go for the Lord wherever He would send. Isaiah heard and volunteered to go anywhere. Then God called him to a specific work for a specific people.

God does not tell us what He wants us to do before we decide whether we will do it. We must accept God's will for our lives "sight unseen" before He will make clear to us what that will is. When we have honestly yielded everything to Him, and only then, He will make us know what we are to do.

God Speaks Through Prayerful Consideration

There is a very real sense in which this full surrender to the will of God settles everything and guarantees that we shall not make any mistake when the time comes to take the first step in carrying out His will. If you are honestly willing to do whatever God wants, then you can be sure He will show you what He wants.

However, this does not do away with the need for prayerful consideration, guided by the Bible and the Holy Spirit, of all the circumstances involved as you seek to arrive at the understanding of God's will. It is just in this way that God usually speaks to us.

Do Not Be Passive

In this regard it would be helpful to realize that we are not to maintain a passive or neutral attitude toward the place of service God has for us, as though we would make no assumption whatever until God tells us what to do. We are not simply to stand idle, waiting to see which way God will point. Rather the Scripture indicates that the place of greatest need should be faced first. Surely the mission field with its millions still waiting their first chance to hear the Gospel is that place of greatest need.

Perhaps you have been looking at things about like this: "Unless God calls me to the mission field I will stay at home." Would it not be more proper to say: "Unless God calls me to stay at home, I will go to the mission field?" This is not to do away with the fact that we should have a definite missionary call before going to the field, but it is a practical way of facing the place of greatest need and thus putting yourself squarely in the way where God can give you a call if it is His will for you to go.

Unless God has made perfectly clear in some way that He does not want you on the mission field, every young Christian should face in that direction, and hold the matter before God until He either leads out to the field or closes the door by a call to other service. If God does call to service in the home field, this is, of course, just as high and blessed a call as the call others may receive to the foreign field.

Above all things, remember that unless we have obeyed the will of God in carrying out the Great Commission of our Lord in whatever way and place He designates, men will perish, and God will require their blood at our hands. Nothing matters quite so much as being able to say with Paul, "I am pure from the blood of all men" (Acts 20:26).

"Then said I, Here am I; send me. And he said, Go, and tell this people."

XI

BUILDING A MISSIONARY PROGRAM
Frank C. Torrey

Missions is native to the local church. The Bible-revealed
unit of Christian activity is the local church. Following the
". . . great persecution against the church which was at Jerusalem, and they were all scattered abroad throughout the regions
of Judea and Samaria . . . Therefore they that were scattered
abroad went everywhere preaching the word" (Acts 8:1, 4).
Out of this compelled ministry came the church at Antioch of
Syria (Acts 11:19). Barnabas was sent by the church at Jerusalem to visit and assist this new Christian center. Having
ministered to the extent of his ability he sought Paul in Tarsus,
and finding him, brought him to Antioch. One year later this
newly established testimony had become mature in doctrine,
spiritual in life, and centered in the person of the Lord Jesus
Christ. It was rich in men of God, taught and concerned, called
"prophets and teachers"; men who, themselves redeemed by the
blood of Christ, were beholding through the eyes of God the
field white unto harvest — a world of lost men.

Perhaps unwittingly, they were constrained by the love of
Christ and fired with the spirit of His final command. Before
His ascension He said, "Go ye into all the world and preach
the gospel to every creature" (Mark 16:15), and as Luke re-
cords it in Acts 1:8, "Ye shall be witnesses unto me both in

FRANK C. TORREY, as pastor of the Calvary Independent Church, Lancaster,
Pa., has through the years been a great friend of World Missions and missionaries. He has toured the foreign mission fields with rich blessing. He has
conducted a unique annual Missionary Conference in his church geared pri-
marily for missionaries themselves, entertaining approximately one hundred
missionaries at each conference. He is well known as a real missionary pastor.

Jerusalem, and in all Judea, and in Samaria, and unto the uttermost part of the earth." Little wonder that to such a people the Holy Spirit turned to set apart certain men for a missionary ministry (Acts 13:1, 2). It was the local church that provided laborers for the harvest field. So it is today, and so will it be as long as the church is on earth.

There was a sensitiveness to the will of God, a "subjection unto the gospel of Christ" which enabled them to hear the Spirit's voice, so that "when they had fasted and prayed, and laid their hands on them, they sent them away." Our Lord Jesus Christ said, as He submitted Himself to God the Father, "I delight to do thy will, O God." Apart from this God never could have said, "Thou art my beloved Son; in thee I am well pleased." Until that same spirit of happy obedience lays its hand upon God-called, and God-directed, and God-equipped young men and women for missionary service, the local church remains, whatever else may be said about it, not fully pleasing to God.

Nor may we overlook the beautiful unity of action revealed in the words, "So they, being sent forth by the Holy Ghost, departed. . ." This working together with God may be as fully experienced today as it was in the days of old. I repeat the introductory statement: missions is native to the local church. The church at Antioch becomes the prototype. God would have the churches of today patterned according to this glorious example.

It is the writer's concern that the foregoing reveal two things: the Bible as the basis of missionary activity; and the local church the divinely-appointed unit in carrying forward the missionary program.

Speaking to the Ephesian elders, the apostle Paul reminds them of their responsibility "to all the flock, over the which the Holy Ghost hath made you overseers. . ." To the church in Thessalonica Paul exhorts the brethren "to know them which labor among you, and are over you in the Lord, and admonish you; and to esteem them very highly in love for their works sake." This interrelation is most important between pastor and people; there is mutual responsibility. The pastor must be a godly leader; the people must give loving response. If the pastor is a man of vision, so also will the people be. Like father, like son; like pastor, like people. The pastor is the key to the missionary program in the local church. He must clearly discern that men without Christ are lost, and be constrained by the love of God for their salvation, and what he discerns he must teach his people. They, with him, must behold the field which is white unto harvest, and as Jesus Christ, be moved with compassion on them.

Let us now consider the ways and means by which a local church may quicken the interest of the people in a definite missionary program. We shall assume that the church has an acquaintance with one or more approved missionary societies. There are many such, operating in practically every country the world over. The pastor and official body of the church, or the pastor and a missionary secretary or missionary committee, would do well to prayerfully outline a simple course of procedure by which a missionary program may be pursued. Three things are essential: information, prayer and action. A mission board secretary will gladly meet with such a group and lay before them a field or fields. Where there is a desire on the part of the church for active partnership in the gospel ministry the mission secretary can present definite ways by which this may be done. There is the perennial and urgent need for prayer. Informed people are praying people. There is the need for material support. This can be general; i.e., to the mission as an organization, or it can be specific in the support of an individual missionary. Much personal interest develops through the latter method, but both are necessary.

If the local church does not have one of its own members on the mission field, pray that such may soon be the case. Nothing arouses more enthusiasm than this. In this way your own particular testimony is extended to the regions beyond.

I. The Pastor and Missions

Under the guidance of the pastor, partiality for field or missionary can be avoided. His own unbiased concern for the welfare and ministry of the worker in the homeland as well as for the laborer in India, China, or Africa, will set an example which the spiritually-minded of his people will readily follow.

The prayer meeting service is the ideal time for the reading of letters from the field. Specific requests for prayer can be emphasized. In this way prayer interest is quickened and those who attend are taught to appreciate in a new way the value of intercession. The name or names of the church's missionaries should never fail to be brought into the pastor's prayer at the morning service on the Lord's day. Organized prayer bands covering the mission fields of the world will undergird the work at home and the missionary on the field. Missions is God's work and prayer moves the arm of God.

Furlough time affords excellent opportunity to bring missionary and people together. A fresh glimpse of the field is seen. A new burden for the unsaved is laid upon hearts. There is a revived stimulus to pray. Young people hear of the need for more workers. Lives are dedicated and the missionary program grows.

II. The Bible School and Missions

The educational program on missions and mission fields, is nowhere more productive than in the church Bible school. Every department through the high school age should be well acquainted with the missionary and his field. Two offering envelopes should be provided, one for the Bible school fund and the second for the missionary fund. The scholars should be taught to pray for the missionary by name. His picture, and one of his house, and a third of the people among whom he works, should hang in the assembly room. Correspondence should be carried on either by the department superintendent or someone appointed to this privileged task.

The classes above the high school age should have class interest in a missionary, and in due time each class should undertake the support of a missionary. As the missionary family grows the entire school can contribute to the missionary fund, and this augmented by monies from other sources in the church, can carry the missionary program.

It will be found that as the missionary interest grows, so also will the church grow and the local activities increase.

III. THE YOUNG PEOPLE AND MISSIONS

Young people's groups are usually enthusiastic in cooperation with a definite program of missions. Possible projects are continually arising. A missionary needs equipment for outgoing. Items such as a typewriter, baggage, camera, microscope for hospital laboratory work, watch, books, etc., are splendid responsibilities for such groups to assume. There should be occasional missionary speakers. Challenging books on missionary biography and experience should be available.

Ladies' groups can prepare bandages, make children's clothing and many useful articles for the everyday demand of the mission field.

Each missionary has his circle of friends and praying partners outside the church family. This means a mailing. The church should make itself responsible for the multigraphing and mailing of this letter.

Adjuncts to missionary interest are: an attractive map with tiny lights brought through from the back indicating the field of service of each worker; well-taken pictures mounted uniformly and of uniform size hung where the congregation may be reminded of their missionary responsibility; interesting literature from the missions involved and an adequate supply of the mission's magazine.

IV. THE MISSIONARY CONFERENCE

Then there is the missionary conference. Nowhere can the atmosphere of missions be better found than in the fellowship of a half dozen or more missionaries brought together to rehearse all that God has done with them and how He has

opened the door of faith unto the Gentiles. Set apart a few
days annually for this purpose. Begin with no less than three
days and increase it to a full week or eight days. Your mission
societies will be glad to cooperate. A well-chosen group of missionaries representing several world fields; a carefully planned
program; the avoidance of monotony of procedure; the effort
to bring as many as possible of old and young into direct contact with the workers and their fields — all these will be of
untold value.

Encourage the opening of homes for the entertainment of
your missionary guests. Personal contact in the intimacy of the
home has formed lasting friendships. Children growing up in
such a home look upon the missionary and mission work as part
of a normal Christian ministry. Mutual intercessory prayer
flows out of such hospitality. Through such contacts God speaks
and only eternity will reveal the blessed results.

A word must be said about finances. Liberal giving is the
fruit of a Bible-taught, world-informed, and Spirit-controlled
Christian life. Just as informed people are praying people, so
also are the people who give. The Word of God is filled with
passages which are an encouragement to giving, i.e., the eighth
and ninth chapters of II Corinthians). These are among the
most compelling passages in the New Testament. Speaking of
the manifold blessings in the ministry of giving, the apostle
Paul says in II Corinthians 9:12-15: "For the administration
of this service not only supplieth the want of the saints, but is
abundant also by many thanksgivings unto God; Whiles by the
experiment of this ministration they glorify God for your pro-
fessed subjection unto the gospel of Christ, and for your liberal
distribution unto them, and unto all men; And by their prayer
for you, which long after you for the exceeding grace of God in
you." Maintained interest results in maintained giving. It is
well for the church to adjust itself to the financial policy of
each mission organization, and to contribute to the missionary
through the society.

Finally, let us be reminded that the whole missionary program is based upon the Word of God. When in the eighth chapter of Nehemiah, the people gathered at the water gate and clamored for the "book of the law of Moses," a pulpit was made on which Ezra and his companions stood. "They read in the book in the law of God distinctly, and gave the sense, and caused them to understand the reading . . . then he (Nehemiah) said unto them, Go your way, eat the fat, and drink the sweet, and send portions unto them for whom nothing is prepared: . . . and all the people went their way to eat, and to drink, and to send portions, . . . because they had understood the words that were declared unto them" (Nehemiah 8:8, 10, 12).

This church age is drawing to a close. Practically one-half the world has yet to hear the Gospel. Our Lord Jesus said, "The harvest truly is plenteous, but the labourers are few; pray ye therefore the Lord of the harvest, that he will send forth labourers into his harvest" (Matthew 9:37, 38).